HOW TO SELL PRODUCTS AND SERVICES WITH

MOBILE APPS

THE BLUEPRINT TO MARKETING ON 5.4 BILLION MOBILE DEVICES

MAURICE UFITUWE

Published by
Ecommerce Maurice Victor
Bonn, Federal Republic of Germany

Ecommerce
Maurice Victor

New York ▪ Paris ▪ London
Tokyo ▪ Berlin

Disclaimer and Terms of Use: The Author and Publisher has strived to be as accurate and complete as possible in the creation of this book, notwithstanding the fact that he does not warrant or represent at any time that the contents within are accurate due to the rapidly changing nature of the Internet. While all attempts have been made to verify information provided in this publication, the Author and Publisher assumes no responsibility for errors, omissions, or contrary interpretation of the subject matter herein. Any perceived slights of specific persons, peoples, or organizations are unintentional. In practical advice books, like anything else in life, there are no guarantees of income made. Readers are cautioned to reply on their own judgment about their individual circumstances to act accordingly. This book is not intended for use as a source of legal, business, accounting or financial advice. All readers are advised to seek services of competent professionals in legal, business, accounting, and finance field.

First Printing, 2015
ISBN: 978-3-00-050819-6

Published by:

Ecommerce Maurice Victor
Grubenstr. 69A
53179 Bonn, Federal Republic of Germany
Printed in Germany

This book is dedicated to startups, local businesses, entrepreneurs and professionals in the trenches fighting to keep their dreams alive.

"If your plans don't include mobile, your plans are not finished."
– Wendy Clark, Coca-Cola

"If you're not using mobile marketing to attract new customers to your business, don't worry — your competitors are already using it and are getting those customers instead."
– Jamie Turner, 60SecondMarketer.com

"The two parts of technology that lower the threshold for activism and technology is the Internet and the mobile phone. Anyone who has a cause can now mobilize very quickly."
– Howard Rheingold, author

"The mobile phone is used from when you get up in the morning and is often the last thing you interact with at night."
– Jan Chipchase, Frog Design

Praise for "How to Sell Products and Services with Mobile Apps" by Maurice Ufituwe

★★★★★

"I searched for a while for tips and information on using mobile apps to sell my products to my customers. Most information I found was useless and anyone who claimed to be an expert wanted a fortune just to show me how it's done. I know there are businesses that use apps for their marketing; however I was not knowledgeable of how this was done. Then when I read this book the light turned on, I was so happy I learned some new information I could use in my business.

It's hard enough for a business to succeed today and everything is expensive. This book delivered just what I needed! It opened my mind to new horizons and opportunities I never thought were possible. There is lots of useful information including how to use apps, how they can help your business make money, how to connect with your customers, how to do market research and how to get started with an app.

Apps are the future of business and you need this kind of information to get your business set up to take advantage of the opportunity to reach potentially millions of users worldwide. Great book!"

Simply Sue

★★★★★

"This is a great way for someone like me who is new to selling with your phone. Gives all the basic strategies and guides you in the right direction to making sales on the web. Highly recommend."

Charles Seagraves

★★★★★

"I'll admit, I'm 'old-school' all the way, hate this world of technology. That being said, and the world still spinning, retail is getting killed by online shopping - so either get an app or go broke! Found this very enlightening as another approach to selling things or services. Worth the read, can always learn something new."

D. Takao

★★★★★

"Super handy "how to book"! Great read and highly suggest getting it NOW! I appreciate the simple and easy to read format."

Judy Dobberpuhl

How to Sell Products and Services with

MOBILE APPS

The Blueprint to Marketing on 5.4 Billion Mobile Devices

<u>Download the eBook on your Amazon Kindle Device</u>:
http://www.amazon.com/dp/B00C007EUM

Bonus: How to Get an iPhone for Free

Learn the secrets to getting your first iPhone shipped to your doorstep within few days. Get your hands on your first Smartphone for FREE today.

viii

Table of Contents

Preface

Welcome and thank you for buying this book! I'm really excited about it. This shows me that you value this information and are truly interested in learning how apps can make you money, turn your business around, increase sales, and build strong relationships with your customers.

This book was created with the intent of showing entrepreneurs and local businesses how to tap into the growing trend the app phenomenon has created since the launch of the iPhone in 2007. I believe it will greatly benefit savvy entrepreneurs and local businesses that seize the opportunity of this development, as it is a market movement they should pay close attention to for many years to come. I believe apps will transform the retail landscape radically and, looking back five years from now, many businesses will notice a significant change in their day-to-day dealings in terms of sales and lead generation. Many will even wonder how they were capable of doing business before mobile apps came to fruition.

This is the biggest revolution that has occurred since Gutenberg's printing press in 1438, one that transcends the casual business-customer relationship, solves business needs, and maximizes the response rates while minimizing the risks of loss in a very decisive way. I hope you'll both enjoy reading this book and learn new things that you can potentially implement in your business. If you have questions related to apps, Mobile Marketing, and Internet Marketing, your feedback is greatly appreciated. Please get in touch with us and we will strive to answer all your inquiries.

How This Book Was Born

How was this book born? Originally, when I started working on this book, the intent was to educate businesses on the functionalities of mobile apps and how they could benefit from them and their sales. The information I put together was limited to a simple 18 page PDF report, explaining the basics of app marketing so that businesses could make an informed decision before buying an app. I'd create a mockup app when contacting businesses and send them the report explaining how the app works and how it benefits them.

A lot of businesses I talked to surprisingly had no idea about app marketing and what the benefits of an app in their sales funnel were. How could they have been aware when 99% of the time apps are downloaded for other purposes than selling apple pies, drinks and other produce for daily consumption? Soon after, I came to the realization that I had to develop the report with a marketing angle rather than just showing the functionalities. The PDF report grew astoundingly from 18 pages in December 2012 to 40 pages in March 2013, and consequently, to 100 pages in the course of 10 months. I soon discovered authorship skills that surprisingly were present but lay dormant within me. The process was a lot of fun, challenging, very creative and very inspiring; I've enjoyed it every step of the way.

My journey as an entrepreneur and business owner started with Internet Marketing and evolved today into Mobile Apps and Marketing. I hope many books will follow in the footsteps of this one. *"How to Sell Products and Services with Mobile Apps"* is available in both eBook and paperback format. It is not just a print book; it is a multichannel interactive guide to the world of apps and Mobile Marketing. You can use your cell phone to interact with the book. Lastly, you can use social media

to interact with me and other users. The contact information is provided at the end of the book.

This book will be updated with new information as the technology evolves and as new sales methods come along the way. You may consult with us for quotes, sales, strategy, and ideas implementation regarding apps, Mobile Marketing, Internet Marketing and Social Media by submitting a ticket to our support team at support [at] appsolutemarketingx.com.

Yours for more profits,
Maurice Ufituwe

Updated August, 2016 & January, 2020.

Whom This Information Is For:

Hotels
Restaurants
Pizzas
Taxis
Bars
Nightclubs
DJs
Music Bands
Event Organizers
Lounges
Cafes
Hair Salons
Manicures
Barber Shops
Doctors
Dentists
Chiropractors
Health Clubs
Gyms
Lawyers
Accountants

Financial Services
Jewelers
Realtors
Shop Owners
Non-Governmental Organizations (NGOs)
Churches

PART ONE: MOBILE APPS & MOBILE MARKETING

In this section, we show how technology is reshaping marketing. We delineate how mobile apps work in your sales funnel and how they are used to generate leads and retain customers.

Why Businesses Need Mobile Apps

Are business apps for real and why should we pay attention to them? Are they here to stay, or are they gadgets and gizmos just like the Tamagotchi was in the '90s?

Mobile is the 7th media. The first mass media in the history of mankind was Gutenberg's printing press in 1438. Some 500 years later, the second mass media emerged at about 1900 as recordings. The first recordings were "clay" records, eventually shifting that media to vinyl and then to digital formats. The third mass media is the cinema, which followed about 10 years later. Today's 3D motion pictures with THX HD-Dolby Surround sound systems are a far cry from the early black and white subtitled movies. The fourth mass media, the radio, also appeared very close to that time, essentially around 1920. Radio was the first broadcast media, where the consumption was a "streaming" concept.

The fifth mass media is the biggest and most dominant in our culture today: TV. Introduced to the mass market in about 1950, TV didn't really introduce anything new that had not already existed because we had multimedia in the cinema, and broadcast in radio. The Internet, the sixth mass media, saw its debut in the 1990s. The Internet is a personal media; however, it is not very mobile because most of the activities are done whilst seated in a fixed place (Source: Mobile as 7th of the Mass Media, Tomi Ahonen). In its humble beginnings, the mobile phone was only a clunky voice device for the masses through the 1990s. It later emerged as a mass media outlet with WAP, I-Mode and premium SMS around the year 2000.

With 2G, 3G, and next generation, mobile attributes evolved into sending and receiving data such as faxes, pictures and videos through MMS, and mobile phones are now heavily used for data communications such as SMS messages, browsing mobile websites, and even streaming audio and video files. However, its biggest achievement is that it has created in just 15 years a single market with 5.4 billion buyers around the world, a market far bigger than Facebook, Google, China, the EU, or the US.

Gutenberg & The Printing Press

When Gutenberg envisioned the printing press, he had automation in mind. Little did he know that his invention would spark a revolution in the hearts and minds of people that would transform society and civilization radically in fields such as education, religion, literature, commerce, politics, health, science, marketing and advertising, just to name a few. Up until then book printing was done manually. This was very labor intense, and a painstaking task that took years for the production of just a handful of copies. Mass production was a foreign concept yet to be discovered. Monks, scribes, scholars, and masters in their fields handwrote them with great care.

There were around 30,000 books in all of Europe before Gutenberg's press. Less than 50 years later that figure jumped to 12 million. When the printing press came along with millions of people having access to knowledge, it overthrew the feudal system. The clergy and the powers that be were not amused with the sudden societal changes. Mobile apps take the printing press to a whole new level where physical boundaries between humans have literally vanished. Gutenberg's printing press was a catalyst to the renaissance movement in Europe; let's see where the continuous usage of mobile apps takes the society to in the 21st century.

Mobile apps and cyberspace are reshaping culture, society and the human experience on multiple fronts in a very profound way. Trade, marketing and E-commerce are leading the way in this global, planetary, technological and revolutionary transformation. It is expedient to consider each mobile device on the planet as an extended sales agent working for you, a finite piece of land that needs to be conquered by all necessary means, or a piece of real estate to credit your bank account every month with payment from rent.

Mobile apps and Mobile Marketing are the last frontier in marketing to solve much of the limitations; businesses have lingered on for far too long in the economic society. They bridge the gap. The big takeaway you will learn from this book is that nothing is impossible in the virtual world. The only limitation you will ever have on your journey to success is your own imagination and creativity to conceptualize and envision things. You are venturing into a universe where you can basically dictate the rules of engagement.

The Missing Link
The question is how do you tap into this huge global market of 5.4 billion buyers for your most needed benefit? The answer is pretty obvious, you basically need 2 things: traffic, and some kind of device to drive sales and manage customers on mobile phones. Websites and mobile apps are the front and back end of your business on mobile devices. Everyone knows that money is made on the back end, not from the first sale but from multiple sales. A website is simply a lead magnet pointing customers towards your business. Yet, up until now retaining these customers from going elsewhere has often been a challenge few businesses were capable to deal with. So, how do you keep those eyeballs from leaving your space, and migrating elsewhere? Customer retention is essential, this is the bedrock of your business, the key to your success; we shall address this

question thoroughly during the course of this book and that's precisely where a mobile app comes in pretty handy.

Front End & Back End

There's a lot of confusion and a misguided debate surrounding whether businesses should have a website rather than a mobile app, or vice versa. This debate suffers from myopia because from a marketing point of view, they complement each other, they need each other; one cannot live without the other. One is a lead generation system, while the other is a customer relationship management system. The two are a perfect match.

Just like you need a cocktail of drugs and therapies such as chemotherapy, hormone therapies, biological therapies, etc., to treat cancer, you need both a website and a mobile app to supercharge sales on mobile devices. There are 5.4 billion mobile devices on the planet; this technology will eventually replace PCs and notebooks and is expected to only grow stronger.

Businesses can harness the potential of this huge market through invitation only when customers grant them permission to market and build rapport through devices such as mobile apps. Mobile apps are the missing link, the missing ingredient, the last puzzle businesses have repeatedly emulated for eons to dial customers back inside their business with dismal and pathetic results. The time has come, the wait is over; the sales cycle has now come full circle with the final stepping stone falling into place. The jigsaw puzzle is solved.

Foot Traffic

Customer Retention

Prior to the surge of apps and mobile devices, businesses had no control and relied heavily on phone calls, leaflets, flyers, ads, postcards, letters, word of mouth advertisement and whatever ploy they could think of to manage the back end and to reach out to their target audience. These century old marketing methods for customer relationship management system had a major fundamental flaw built in; they all lack a feedback mechanism that would afford businesses a greater control to yield higher returns and steer their marketing in the right direction.

This is how the back end was managed for good or bad with much limitation. It's like climbing a stiff mountain or worse a roof top with blinded eyes and both hands tied up with nothing to hold onto, to prevent a fall. To use a more accurate analogy that best describes the rough terrain, they had to navigate through to obtain their goal. Not the best and ideal situations in my opinion, however, what other choice did they really have?

Fig. 1.1 Lead Generation in the 1800s

If a business owner was running a special offer his customers were interested in, he had nothing tangible such as telephone number, street address or email address to let them know about this super offer. His best bet was word of mouth advertisement, or simply to wait for their second visit. This struggle however, has come to rest. These subterfuges and shenanigans businesses had to endure for far too long are things of the past. A tectonic shift of great magnitude we have, yet it is silent to feel its full impact, but surely taking over in the retail environment. There is no looking back, a new paradigm shift — one that is shaking up the old business model from the ground, giving small and midsized businesses more leverage, more options, thereby encouraging flexibilities. The trend is irreversible, a new chapter is being written.

Business apps connect businesses and customers. When a customer walks inside your business, this gives you the opportunity to send him offers via text messaging, allowing you to deepen your relationship with him once he has downloaded your app. No more predicaments, all these impediments are cut out. A mobile website in comparison is not capable of doing that. Mobile websites are dull and sterile in many respects. Since the advent of mobile devices and mobile apps, things have slightly changed for the better. Gone are the days of total

8

uncertainty; of those tough times when you wished you had more clients. Apps are like a breath of fresh air, they are far more predictable than any other type of advertisement you had at your disposal in the past. They are comparable to a website on steroids, reminding customers about your business constantly, saving them the hassle of surfing the Web and searching for your competitors. While print media is static and boring, apps are fresh, dynamic, and interactive! They literally charge up your business by creating a familiar, cozy, warm rapport with customers, like some sort of magical connection one was lacking until now. None of the previous advertising platforms — be it TV, radio, or even landline telephone — were capable of duplicating this and due to these unique attributes, they have literally transformed the landscape of retail in a very profound way and the way we run businesses forever.

Instant Feedback

Apps bring customers and businesses closer to one another, they allow information to flow seamlessly and much faster between the two, and because of this instant feedback, the renewal of stock is quickened. The benefit to the seller is increased as more depreciation of fixed storage costs can be spread over a larger number of units sold in a relatively short period of time. Nothing goes to waste, the capital invested is more profitable as a result, and the consumer is informed much faster about the deals they can take advantage of. This is groundbreaking! It's a new line of communication (comparable to the Washington-Moscow Direct Communications Link[1]) between businesses and consumers that circumvents traditional advertising channels, saves costs, and cuts short the amount of time needed to deliver goods and services to a clientele desperately looking for them.

Gone is the misfortune of restaurants, for instance: when they had to figure out ways to fill tables on slow days, and both perishable and non-perishable inventories had to go to waste as a result of sitting too long on store shelves. A new dawn in

---

[1] The Washington-Moscow Direct Communications Link referred to as the Moscow-Washington hotline, or "red telephone" is a system that allows direct communication between the leaders of the United States and Russia. This hotline was established in 1963 during the Cold War and links the White House with the Pentagon and the Kremlin.

the age of digital marketing has arrived, one that combines the functionalities of images, text, audio, video, and social media to reach out to their audience any time they want.

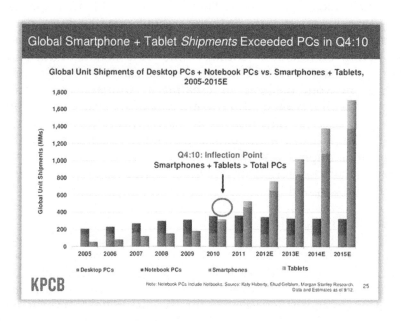

Fig. 1.2[2] Global Unit Shipments of Desktop PCs & Notebook PCs vs. Smartphones & Tablets, 2005-2015E

Ad Revenues
The increase in Smartphone and tablet usage has created a bigger market than TV, print, and radio combined. The era of desktop PCs, which was instrumental for the rise of the Internet, has peaked and is paving the way for smaller portable devices, which are now affordable to the masses on a global scale. They also require less cost to maintain and run. This shift in technology is indicative of where the advertising money will be spent in the years to come in terms of sales and lead generation.

In 2011, mobile advertising spending in the US reached $1.45 billion; it was up 89% from $769.6 million in 2010. Worldwide ad spending was 3 times that of the US with $2.34

---

[2] Source: http://www.slideshare.net/kleinerperkins/2012-kpcb-internet-trends-yearend-update

billion in 2010 and $4.08 billion in 2011. 2012 saw the biggest spike in sales with a 180% record increase to $4.06 billion for the US, and sales worldwide for the same year doubled at $8.761 billion with a 119.5% increase. In 2013, mobile ad spending grew 105% worldwide to $17.96 billion and in the US those figures were $8.04 billion. Ad spending was an estimate $31.45 billion worldwide in 2014 with the US believed to be at $17.73 billion. Fast forward 4 years from now and mobile is poised to grow by 86% by 2018 to over $33 billion for the US. Sales worldwide are expected to reach $94 billion for the same year (Source: eMarketer March 2014).

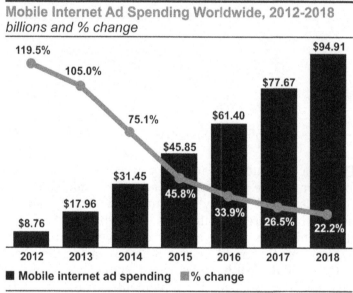

Fig. 1.3[3] US Mobile Ad Spending Worldwide, 2012 – 2018 (Billions and % Change)

---

[3] Source: http://www.emarketer.com/Article/Driven-by-Facebook-Google-Mobile-Ad-Market-Soars-10537-2013/1010690

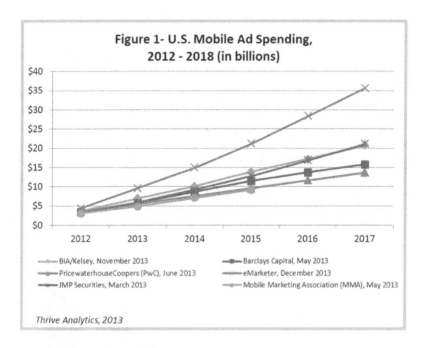

Fig. 1.4⁴ US Mobile Ad Spending, 2012 – 2018 (in Billions)

This is a very lucrative market you can tap into when you enable your mobile app to receive ads. You could run ads that are congruent and thereby cater to the needs of your target audience, thus increasing the click-through rate. A nightclub, event organizer, or a local bar, for example, could run beverage, music, music bands, or ring tone ads inside their mobile app. Gyms and health clubs could sponsor ads for sport brands, sport resorts, food, supplements, drugs or anything that's health and wealth related. Taxis could target car dealership ads, hotel, airline, restaurant and retail shop ads. Similarly, a Cuban restaurant in West Palm Beach, Florida or elsewhere in the world could run ads for Cuban cigars, Cuban rum, Cuban music or Cuban vacations to Havana to their clientele, and the list goes on.

In 2011, 6.3% of all local online advertising was served on a mobile device. That was significantly low compared to TV, the Internet, radio and print, which were the dominant force for advertising. In just 4 years those figures have flipped to mo-

---

⁴ Source: http://www.thriveanalytics.com/blog/?p=189

bile, allowing businesses and individuals to get their share of the pie that was once reserved for traditional media outlets, but is now an open market and a money-making opportunity for everyone with a downloadable app. According to the next chart below, by 2016, 88% of all local online advertising will be served up on a mobile device. These are interesting times, because this shows the pie will grow even bigger. Not having a mobile app to take advantage of the spending spree would be quite frankly an ill-advised and a wasted opportunity. This is passive income any business could surely benefit from and be able to funnel money back into other parts of their business, such as marketing, inventory, personnel, infrastructure, research and development, or just use it to cover basic utility expenses.

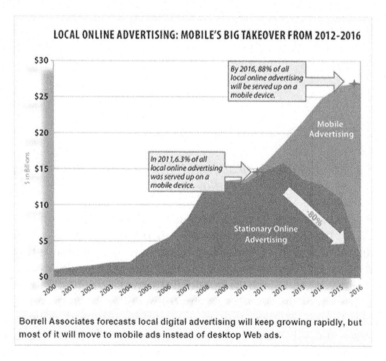

Fig. 1.5[5] Local Online Advertising in the US: Mobile's Big Takeover from 2012-2016, A Forecast

[5] Source: http://www.poynter.org/news/mediawire/153153/forecast-local-ad-spending-on-web-mobile-to-overtake-newspapers-by-2013

Viral Apps

Another reason to consider selling your business on mobile is its viral nature. Mobile is more viral than the Internet, TV, print, or radio. It is also highly targeted, and converts much better than traditional media outlets.

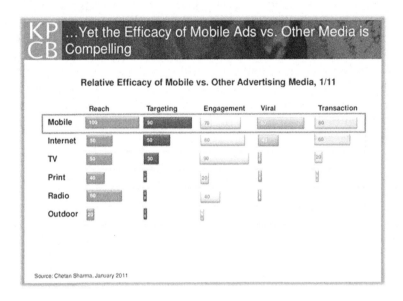

Fig. 1.6[6] Relative Efficacy of Mobile vs. Other Advertising Media, 01/2011

A viral app has purpose because it slashes costs considerably. It brings more referrals through word of mouth advertising and it is a great income generator. The more downloads you get, the more your income will soar, and conversely the less you will have to spend on advertisements. This is a win-win situation, a path you can follow to grow your audience rather than just throwing money onto outbound advertisements you can't tweak and track — no one really pays attention to those and they convert less. Imagine one of your friends needs plumbing services; he needs the hot tub, or some filters cleaned fast. He asks you for help; if you know any good plumber in the neighborhood who will get the job done. You

[6] Source: http://www.slideshare.net/kleinerperkins/kpcb-top-10-mobile-trends-feb-2011

say yes, I know Joe the plumber on Riverside Ave because you happen to be one of his clients. He asks for his phone number and you decide to share his app instead. That's because Joe's app lets you share his app with other users by email, Facebook, Twitter or SMS. He says yes let me have it and the minute you press the share button, you magically converted your friend into one of Joe's new disciples, unbeknownst to Joe the plumber and his plumbing services. Now Joe has new downloads, a new source of income, less to spend on advertising and a customer for life. If Joe impresses your friend, he will refer the cool app to other users too. This is just one example. However, getting your app to spread faster than celebrity gossip takes a lot more than bolting on some Twitter and Facebook buttons. It requires strategizing a world of social interaction inside your app.

Viral ability is about interacting with people and enticing them to participate, and it can be built into your app from the beginning. First and foremost, your app has to have something valuable to share. That something could be a coupon, a gift, a special offer, a photo, a great wine, a free massage, an article, a free report, a slogan, a quote, a song, a Bible verse, a special event, a personal experience, a cause, political activism, an idea, a concept, something really abstract, or anything else of great value.

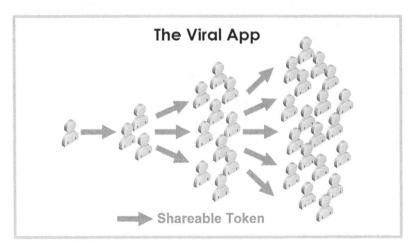

The Viral App

➡ Shareable Token

It's your customer's little pride and joy, and it has to be shareable. You could think of something that's very personal to

15

you and your business that you know will create a strong connection with customers; this is the perfect lead magnet that will thrust sales in your business! Giving freebies away people will be excited to take advantage of and share with others is a good way to pre-sell them on much bigger items.

Second, inviting friends and connecting with others should be a part of their daily usage to grow your business. An example could be, "download the app to get a 30% discount from your first wine purchase," and then you will reward them with a $15 coupon for referring friends and family. Or, you could let people in your nightclub for free when they download your app at the entrance and give them a 5-10% discount on future drinks, per friend invite. You could give free spa massages or manicures to clients in exchange for downloading your app, and reward them with coupons or VIP treatments when they refer friends and family.

Serial entrepreneur Eric Ries, author of the *"Lean Startup,"* a groundbreaking educational book that's turning the conventional wisdom about entrepreneurship on its head, makes the process of starting a company less risky. This is because it favors experimentation over elaborate planning, customer feedback over intuition, and iterative design over traditional "big design up front" development. He shares with us the rules of engagement of a successful viral app — Value, Intuitive, Reward, Ability, and Like-able. The acronym of these elements can be summed up interestingly in one word: *"viral."* So what does it mean? Here's what it all boils down to:

1. Value: You need to be absolutely sure that your app is exactly what your audience needs and that it answers a critical need — and how do you do this? Consumer testing! Constantly test and integrate feedback at every stage of development, so when it becomes release time, you are positive that your target audience will be satisfied with your product. After you release your app, it's not time to stop testing. You should be consistently tweaking your app until your audience can't live without it.

2. Intuitive: Your app needs to have intuitive design, and, more importantly, extremely intuitive sign-up and share functions, to ensure that users don't get frustrated in the beginning

16

stages. Achieve this by making signing in through social media accounts automatic. Today's users don't like mountains of usernames and passwords to remember. And make sure sharing across social media channels is naturally engrained, not hidden.

3. Reward: Reward users with incentives and promotions to encourage them to share and invite friends to join. Uber's recent $20 for referrals and for the new sign-up is one example of a great reward campaign.

4. Awesome: Your app needs to be more than good, useful, and valuable — it has to be awesome. Today's users are cool, and your app needs to be too. Don't think "awesome" is quantifiable when it comes to apps? Think about it — there are countless apps similar to yours, but what separates the fails from the successes is an app that makes the user feel cooler.

Let's look at Instagram. Plenty of other photo editing apps have failed, but Instagram rose to success. Why? Because of its intuitive setup and instructions, the ease of sharing across social networks, its like-ability (both literally and figuratively), the rewards (filtered pictures to make your friends jealous), and because, compared to other apps, it is just, well, awesome.

Instagram

5. Like-able: Sorry, but this is one tip you can't ignore. Your app's brand needs to be likeable, both so users literally like it, and so they can "like" it easily across social media channels. Users liking your app leads to them sharing it with friends.

If, like being awesome, this seems too subjective to you, think about it in target audience terms. What does your audience like? Look at their habits and see what they are sharing and liking across other sectors. Mold your brand accordingly to

17

ensure you are creating a product they don't just need but like, and want to share with others too.[7]

Viral Flow

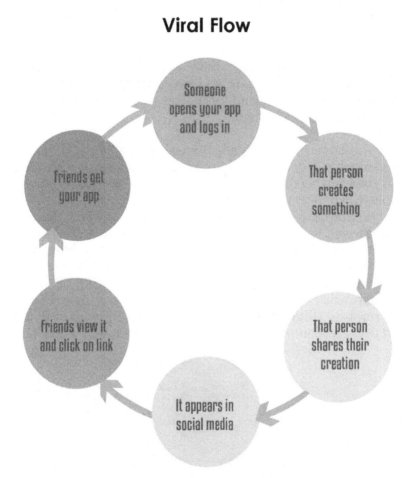

One of the ways to increase your likeability is to pay attention to the needs of your clients, to engage them permanently and to respond to feedbacks. Engagement with mobile is essential; it plays a significant role in generating sales and getting referrals. If you can add features that may not necessarily be relevant to your core activities, but you know are a great bene-

[7] Source: http://www.viralblog.com/viral-social-games/5-tips-to-make-your-app-go-viral/#sthash.XEYT23bd.dpuf

fit to your audience, something that gets them really excited, this will significantly impact your likeability, you should definitely add them.

This is the perfect hook, magnets that will attract people like honey attracts bears, candy bars attract kids, drugs attract crack addicts, protons attract electrons and filth attracts flies. Look at your market, study their behavior and identify patterns they have in common. Look for anything that turns them on, that puts them in a particular mood and that comes close to being an addiction. Brainstorm concepts and ideas that will impress them and that turns out to be a conversation starter with friends and family. This could be a RSS feed to anything streaming inside your app, with text, video and images, quotes you post on a regular basis, ideas to improve their lives, a surprise gift, local and celebrity gossip, news flashes to quizzes and anodyne Tetris games where you or your brand are featured inside, etc. Make your app become a fun, exciting and cool extension of their lives, their habits, what they like, in order to espouse their personalities, of who they are.

Think of the possibilities, the simple yet little ideas that can enhance the users' experience greatly, that can benefit and impact their lives and start implementing them. There are plenty of examples to copy from, so look around you and see what made other apps successful. Use your imagination and be creative, and think out of the box. This is a very exciting and thrilling exercise you can delve into to see how you can add more value to your app. As long as these features keep your audience engaged and they see a benefit of having your app on their devices, this should be your first priority in your mobile strategy. To learn more about hooks and viral features your app can benefit from, please get in touch with us for a quick brainstorming session. The contact information is provided to you at the end of the book.

Why Businesses Are Losing Money on Mobile Devices
From the information above, we can see how vital mobile apps are for businesses. But what else does a business need to market itself successfully on cell phones and tablets? Most businesses are aware that having a website on the Internet is essential. However, how many know that they are being searched on cell phones by savvy customers in their local area, only to switch to the competition when they fail to find them

on mobile devices? If you look at the number of businesses that have a mobile optimized website versus those that don't, you will see the number one cause for revenue loss on mobile devices. Not to mention the frustration of users when they seek answers they can easily find on desktop PCs, yet are absent on mobile devices.

According to a Mashable article[8] posted on October 10th, 2012, mobile traffic in May 2012 made up 10% of global Internet traffic. As indicated in the chart below, more people will use mobile phones rather than PCs to get online, according to a study by Gartner done in 2010. Yet, many businesses have not fully optimized their websites for mobile, thus frustrating visitors with tricky navigation and slow loading times. In May 2013 that figure jumped to 15%, and a year later it was estimated at 25%.

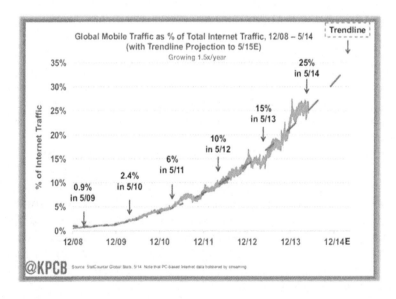

Fig. 1.7[9] Global Mobile Traffic as Percentage of Total Internet Traffic, 12/2008 – 05/2014

In the same article, we read that a survey of major advertisers in early 2011 showed only 21% had launched a mobile-

---

[8] http://mashable.com/2012/10/10/mobile-site-small-business
[9] Source: http://heidicohen.com/state-of-mobile-2014

friendly site. A 2012 L2 study[10] of the top 100 fashion, beauty, retail, hospitality, watch and jewelry brands found that only two-thirds had mobile-optimized sites, and yet a third of those did not allow consumers to shop from their sites. You need to be found on mobile devices and desktop PCs to drive foot traffic and make sales. Your mobile app and your mobile website are the tools you need to make sales on mobile devices.

Desktop Website

Mobile Website

Mobile App

Local Businesses & Mobile Marketing

As a side note, I will add that websites using flash animation need to reconsider this option because their websites do not work on mobile devices. For example, if you type *"file-type:swf restaurant new york"* into your search bar, you will get a list of restaurants in New York City that use flash animation on their websites. You can do the same search for any

---

[10] http://mashable.com/2012/01/11/mobile-commerce-brands-luxury-prestige-l2-study

niche, in any country around the world, and you will find all sorts of businesses that are currently losing money on mobile devices, yet none of these businesses are aware that is seriously hampering their growth onto mobile devices.

A 3rd party survey of 3.5 million web pages revealed that approximately 30-40% of websites contained elements that were driven by Flash, and many consumers are unaware of the technical issues between Apple and Adobe Flash and will assume the website is broken, when they land on your website (Source: AIS Media). These flash animations are great visual enhancements. However, their effectiveness pales in comparison to the money lost because of the technical impediment they pose in terms of sales and traffic.

Flash Error Messages

How Mobile Apps and Mobile Marketing Work

Business apps are downloadable onto your Smartphone, just like any other app in the app stores. A simple scan of a QR code suffices to download the application onto your cell phone in seconds. The other way of getting downloads is to embed it inside your mobile website and rank your mobile website high in the local searches with some basic SEO groundwork.

Business apps have the capability to receive and send text, audio, images, and video, and they also tap into social media. This functionality alone places them above other outbound marketing methods for their interactive usage and viral reach.

This feature is priceless because of the reach businesses have at their disposal to market and interact with groups that are traditionally out of their reach. When a customer tweets about their dinner last night and shares pictures with friends and family on Facebook from the app, this is a good way of getting publicity for your business.

Imagine for one second your customers advertising your products and services to friends for free, without you asking for it! How effective is that? This functionality is a true moneymaker and a true money saver in terms of marketing and advertisement. It will reap you lots of rewards because of these free unsolicited third party messages. These messages are more valuable than any ad you will ever run to lure clients towards your business. If the customer does it not once or twice, but repeatedly, they will spike their interest to a point where they will want to see what your business and the messages are all about, just to quench their lust for curiosity. This is viral marketing and word of mouth advertising at its best, something any business owner could never dream of and would gladly pay for. And, it is priceless!

Fig. 1.8 Restaurant Diner

Fig. 1.9 Nightclub Selfies

This is one way you have at your disposal to increase your exposure and make more sales. You can also engage your customers one-on-one with personalized messages and casual conversations. It's a great way to create a rapport. Try doing that with TV, radio, and your landline telephone!

With your app you can ask questions, respond to queries, and show that you're a real person. You can show that you really care about your customers and that you're not just a random faceless sales representative. Engaging customers one-on-one is not a farfetched marketing ploy and you'd be quite surprised at the response you'd get if your audience senses you are for real and that you are appreciative of their business. You send out good vibrations and they come back tenfold. The process is so fantastical, so phenomenal, so magical, so mystical and instantaneous. No other technology allows harnessing the arcane laws of the universe with clients on a deeper level, triggering an immediate response to drive sales with such reverence and majesty. This amounts to flirting and rhyming with the cosmic laws of the universe and in literature it bears a name, it's called poetry! So get in the habit of rhyming with the universe as often as you wish. Growing and nurturing this rapport is what will eventually keep your customers coming back, consequently bringing in more customers. This is what engagement marketing and a mobile app can do for you.

Business apps give you the power to collect valuable information, which you can use to refine your offers, slash costs, and improve communication or your brand with a simple and casual conversation. If you were to hire an agency just to get this kind of information, it would cost you a fortune and wouldn't be as accurate as the feedback you get first hand by sending out a quick customer satisfaction survey to your clients.

Studies have shown that mobile devices are always in the range of 2 meters 24/7 from the user's presence and SMS texts along with push-notification messages have a 97% open rate compared to only 16% for email. It takes 26 hours for the average person to report a lost wallet and it takes 68 minutes to report a lost phone (Source: Unisys). It takes 90 minutes for the average person to respond to an email, but only 90 seconds for the average person to respond to a text message (Source: CTIA.org). Seventy percent of all mobile searches result in action within 1 hour (Source: Mobile Marketer).

This information alone is enough to educate anyone about the necessity of mobile apps and mobile devices in your sales funnel. Not having one in your sales funnel can be a death sen-

25

tence to a business, especially in slow days and when your business is facing a dire cash-flow situation. From the graph below, you can see how mobile marketing works and the key role a business app plays to generate sales and leads.

Mobile Apps & Mobile Marketing

1. First, people find your business on the Internet or inside mobile website directories.
2. From the direction on the website, they find their way to your business.
3. Once inside your business, they can download your business app onto their cell phones with a simple QR code scan, or they can download it from your mobile website.
4. You have the permission to advertise on their cell phones via SMS or push-notification messages.
5. Your customers can share comments about their buying experience with friends and family on social media.

6. These shares and comments land in other people's feeds virally to create awareness and advertisement to an audience that is usually out of your business reach.

7. From the buzz created around your business, people will start researching your business to see what the hype is all about.

The great thing about business apps is that they can reach out to an audience that is usually out of reach for a local business, thanks to social media. As we learned in the first chapter, mobile apps are more viral than the Internet. The more shares and comments you receive, the more buzz and attention this creates around your business, and the more leads your business will get. The strategy of your app traffic sales funnel will consist of landing them on your mailing list and use social networking sites to expand your reach virally, and drive them inside your business.

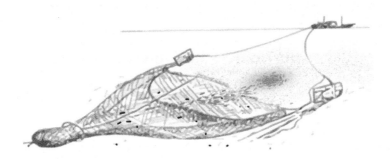

Social Networking Sites

A list is a key asset in your customer relationship management, or CRM in short, to make sales repeatedly and to retain customers on the backend. People think marketing is a number game, but engagement is equally important on social media more than anything else. You need to get followers talking to you and about you on Facebook and Twitter. Again, you can ask questions, respond to queries, and show that you're a real person. You need to connect with them on every level possible with the goal to convert them into sales and generate more leads and referrals. You don't have to pitch them right away. You should avoid coming across as a sales-y person or as worse as a spammer. Nothing turns people off more than that. Instead, be a friend; build rapport, give something of value, show them you're for real, and that you care. Eventually, all this activity and good karma generated by engaging others will spread, go viral, increase your exposure and grow your business.

Social networking sites are just another way of capturing leads like fish nets, and the bottom line of your effort should always focus on list building, lead generation, referrals and making more sales. Our goal when creating our presence and building rapport is not having "20,000 followers" on Twitter or Facebook, like most of us were guilty of when we were caught in the social media frenzy in early 2007. Our goal is to gain real customers and convert them into sales with one-on-one engagement. You are better off with just 50-100 active users spreading your messages, responding to posts and re-tweeting them than having 20,000 who don't have time for you and who couldn't care less about you and your business.

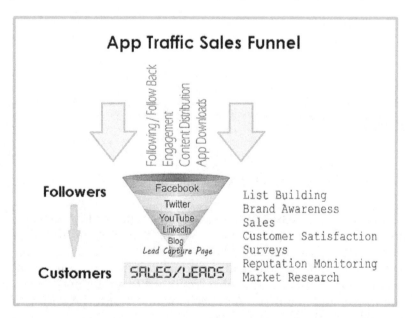

How Can Mobile Apps Help Your Sales?

How can business apps help to increase sales? When you ask this question, you want to know if apps have an intrinsic value in terms of marketing and sales and the answer is definitely, yes! There are four ways businesses can make money with business apps.

The first one is to increase sales with promotional text messages such as special offers, events, coupons, freebies, QR coupons, and through customer satisfaction surveys, etc. This is the primary use of business apps. Second, depending on the number of app downloads you have, you can monetize your apps with ad placements through third parties. The third possibility is to tap into the ad network with banner ads, rich media, video, etc., and the fourth possibility is in-app purchases and upgrades.

Business apps come with a range of functionalities such as loyalty programs, push-notification, voice recorders and cameras, etc., which you can utilize in many ways. When businesses have slow days, for instance, or want more sales, they can:

> ➤ Send "push-notification" messages to give special offers, daily specials, coupons, events, promotions, etc. to customers.
> ➤ Offer redeemable QR coupons to liquidate stocks of unsold inventories, to recoup their initial investment.
> ➤ Post viral messages people will gladly re-post on social networks to increase their exposure.

Moreover, because business apps should be viewed in the long term rather than as a one-off business opportunity, businesses should take advantage of the position they have so that they can build a strong connection with customers. You can build up a regular income, but it all depends on how well you connect and manage your audience, and how congruent and consistent your message is. Here are just a few tips you can use to grow this relationship with them:

> You can update your customers with location-specific information.
> You can send updates about your activities and information about your niche and industry.
> You can update them with timely knowledge, send quizzes or customer satisfaction surveys to get a read of the market, send quotes of the "day," etc.
> You can send ideas for making life easier in the form of advice, tips, recommendations, etc., and ask for feedback.
> You can give financial incentives for taking action.
> You can entertain them by posting viral images on your Facebook fan page, ask them to comment, and ask them to share their personal experiences, post pictures, videos, podcasts, etc., on your blog, website, etc.
> You can host events to product launches, promotions, etc., as then people will re-tweet and share, just to increase your exposure.
> You can ask visitors to share text and video reviews about your business.

As you can see, there are many ways you can connect with your target audience. The key here is interactivity; to create value and a great user experience (UX) people will share and remember for many years with your mobile app. The greater the feedback you get, the more you will be able to see whether or not you're having some impact or not and get some return on your investment. The deeper you can drill into the mindset and psychology of your clients and knowing the "user persona," i.e. the token person you designed the app around, the greater the feedback will be!

User personas in UX designs are snapshots of who the target audience is. They serve for you and your team as a reference point on who you're designing the app for. An example of a user persona is Cathy, a 55-year-old woman. She's your typical waitress, nurse, accountant, florist, or receptionist with a $65,000-$85,000 yearly salary. She's not very tech savvy, she visits Facebook randomly and occasionally, she doesn't have the latest phone, she uses her phone for phone calls, but rarely does she use it when interacting with different apps. She's old school. Another persona is Johnny a 19-year-old tech savvy kid; he's on Snapchat, Reddit, Instagram, Twitch, Twitter, Facebook, Periscope, you name it. He has the latest gadget; he's the typical guy you see in queues waiting for the latest iPhone when it's on sale. This is why an app designed for persona A will be slightly different from an app designed for persona B. The user experience will tank significantly and nosedive if you do not cater to these factors and incorporate them into your designs.

Unlike other platforms, where it's hard to track results of your campaigns, your app can become your eyes and ears of the market based on the feedback you get. If people enjoy using your app, like having it on their mobile devices, can't think of living without it, and believe your app is the best thing that ever was since the invention of the apple pie, this is the testimony to the effect you're having in your marketing campaigns. Your sales will soar as a result. And, as the old adage says (and it still resonates true today), people buy from people they know, like, and trust. In other words, business apps are a great way to increase your likeability and trust with customers, maximizing sales at the same time. You should definitely take advantage of this feature because bonding with customers and creating a cozy and familiar rapport is one way to manage expectations long term and keep them happy, besides providing outstanding products and services.

You can run banner and text ads on mobile devices to drive even more foot traffic inside your business. This is option 3. You need to join an ad network such as Admob, Revmob, Flurry, TapJoy, and countless others to run or receive those ads. To display ads on your app a SDK integration into your app is necessary as this allows ads to run at the top or the bottom of your app layout. SDK stands for software developer's kit and it's a set of programs used to write application programs.

31

Fig. 1.10 Mobile Ads

If an ad pays $2-$5 per 1000 impressions, you can pocket $2000-$5000 off of one campaign with say 100,000 downloads. You need to pick ads that cater to the interests of your users of course to maximize your click through rates; you get paid when an ad gets clicked. This is how making money with the ad networks work. Depending on the products and services you offer, you could provide an upgrade where customers pay a certain amount to get lifetime discounts, premium services, VIP treatments, special bulletins, join exclusive events, etc.

An example of a paid option is a dating app you give away for free, where people show their basic information such as username, picture, age, race, religion and marital status, to meet other people. In the paid version, they get a lot more information such as the full name, job, income, education, hobbies, music, film, sport, figure, type of relationship they want, personal video clips, etc., where users get to know their soulmate a lot better. If your app was downloaded 100,000 times and a third of your clients upgraded to the paid service @ $0.99 or $1.99, you could pocket $29.700 or $59.700 off of this upgrade. You could charge say $100 to $300 for a 15% or 25% lifetime discount, or whatever you see fit. You can up-sell them on as many services as you want and offer them multiple upgrades.

A Little Bit of App History

Here's a quick history of mobile apps and how the app phenomenon started. When Apple launched the iPhone on June 29, 2007, 18 apps were readily available for usage, developed primarily by the Mac maker.

The Apple App Store launched in July 2008, a year after the first iPhone was released, and it had 500 apps. Ten million applications were downloaded in the first weekend of its launch. The Android Market launched a couple months later in October and had 50 apps to start. Research In Motion was not far behind, announcing BlackBerry App World at its developers' conference in October 2008 and accepting submissions from developers in early 2009.

Nokia's Ovi Store opened in 2009, starting its short-lived run as the No. 2 global app store behind Apple's trailblazer. The Windows Phone Marketplace launched in late October 2010. By July 2011, it had nearly 30,000 apps. As of January 2012, it had almost 50,000. The BlackBerry App World had about 37,000 at the end of July 2011. Apple reached the 100,000 app mark first, a little more than a year after launch, in November 2009. Skipping ahead, the Android Market hit 200,000 in early 2011 and nearly doubled its developer output through the remainder of the year. As of now, the market has about 400,000 apps available whereas iOS has over 850,000.

Most of the apps downloaded from the Apple and Android store fall into these categories: Calculate/Utilities, Entertainment, Games, News, Productivity, Social Networking, Sports, and Travel and Weather. None of the apps available for download were business related, meaning that none could sell products and services on mobile devices to users who were downloading them in millions every day. 2012 saw a limited introduction of mobile apps for businesses, which was burgeoning in early 2011 inside the app stores. The trend is expected to further develop in 2015 and grow in the years ahead. As PC usage decreases in favor of mobile devices, mobile apps are expected to fill in the void left behind by traditional business portals and E-commerce platforms.[11]

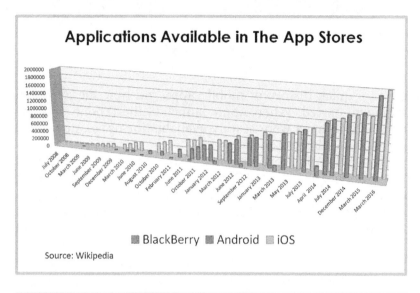

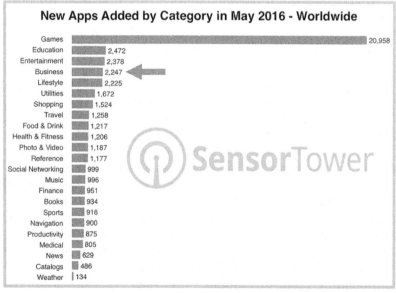

---

[11]http://readwrite.com/2012/02/06/infographic_history_of_mobile_app_s tores#awesm=~okVoByJJvAVLQc

Engagement Marketing vs. Interruption Marketing

There are 3 types of marketing in existence used to land clients: interruption marketing, permission based marketing, and engagement marketing. Prior to the surge of the Internet, social media, and Digital Marketing, advertisement was a one-way alley where a seller could broadcast a message to buyers to sell them products and services. The problem with this antiquated form of advertisement is that you had to craft a message so powerful aimed at the masses and seed it into as many media outlets as possible, primarily TV, radio, and print, hoping to reach your targeted audience in this perilous, often challenging and unpredictable marketing experiment. With many sellers competing for the same space and attention, you had to be resourceful or scream louder than the crowd to get your message across.

This environment created a situation where the brain was constantly bombarded with messages, overloading it with much more information than it could handle. It is said that a typical American is exposed to 30,000 advertising messages a day and when you think about those commercials on TV, radio, billboards, in newspapers, at work and when driving, on buildings, buses, taxis, banners, the logos on cars, trucks, shirts, your computer, your telephone, your home appliances, etc., this is by the stretch of the imagination, no exaggeration. Yet, how effective is this kind of advertisement? How many of these messages influence you in a meaningful way and how many can you remember every day? It's like having hundreds of fishing boats, amassed in one place, over millions and billions of fish, casting nets and catching one or two fish each time. This is a very poor return compared to the resources and time allocated; it's clear this formula doesn't work.

The reason for this poor return is that customers are becoming very good at filtering the noise from the barrage of ads they receive every day, allowing just a few to get through. This phenomenon is called "ad blindness." This phenomenon is exacerbated and perfected to a degree of annoyance when you're immersed in one of your favorite pastimes such as watching soccer, the Super Bowl, live concerts, etc., and you're interrupted with the inevitable blocks of disruptive commercials we are accustomed to, which rob you of your excitement and attention. You're clearly not interested and companies are paying millions to push their products down your throat.

Fig. 1.12 30,000 Advertising Messages

This form of advertising is called interruption marketing because it's the process of finding a prospect generally engaged in something else, like reading a magazine, watching television, watching a game, or driving to work and interrupting them with a commercial message. To do that "creativity" in its conventional form is a huge asset, albeit rare.

Blogger, interactive and digital marketing strategist, *George Benckenstein* wrote the following on his blog, "In citing the example above, if you are not influenced or affected by any one of the 30,000 ad messages a day, how is it that companies keep doing the same thing hoping for a different result? That's insanity." And he adds: "It's also a crap-shoot. It's a matter of broadcasting loud to as many people as possible and hope it trickles down to a potential buyer." He then goes on to say: "As you can see, it's not very effective. For many companies, their solution is to fight clutter with even more clutter. Target audiences, no matter how well segmented, have learned to filter out and ignore the noise. This is a fact..." Benckenstein brings it to the point, but what's the solution?

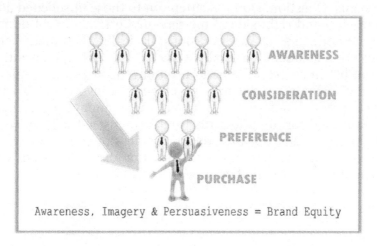

Fig. 1.13 Awareness, Imagery & Persuasiveness = Brand Equity

Permission Marketing
On the other hand, permission marketing, also known as email marketing, consists of emailing you messages you opted in to receive by providing your name and email address in an opt-in box. This type of marketing is the one most commonly used on the Internet. Often, people trade their contact information in exchange for a free report, a free gift, free video, or whatever the case is. This type of advertising has the merit of being less intrusive and more aligned with people's needs and interests than interruption marketing.

One of the first daily tasks an email list subscriber performs consistently, when he turns on his personal computer is to check his inbox for new offers, special reports, insider information, news alerts, etc. before anything else. You don't want to miss out on the latest trend, update, early-bird price dis-

37

counts or whatever you were sent in the wee hours of the night before starting off the day. This is a standard procedure. At least from my end, this is my view and I am sure my situation is no different than that of countless other email subscribers around the globe.

I have 2 separate email accounts where I read my newsletters every day. One runs banner ads at the top and right hand side in my inbox and the other is void of such intrusive commercials. Question: Do I pay attention to those unsolicited ads at the top and right side of my screen? Certainly not, I do ignore them! On some rare occasions; basically when there's not much to read about. Generally, I use to skim through the entire email list in search of beneficial intelligence I can implement in my business or that may be of help to my clients. To be frank I could not care less about those annoying ads that scream loud for attention, that are certainly not aligned with my interests, add no value to my business or cannot increase my knowledge and are a mere distraction of whatever I'm doing in my routine activities.

Fig. 1.14 Permission Marketing

Permission marketing comes in many shapes and forms, such as long sales pages, blogs, video pages, or pop-up windows all with opt-in forms. Unlike interruption marketing like in the case of the banner ads, where there's no end in sight to the unsolicited ad messages broadcasted all day every day, you can opt out any time you want by unsubscribing from your email list; you will receive no more ads, newsletters, or messages.

This form of advertising is superior to traditional offline marketing in the sense that you have more control over the flow of information you want to receive. Businesses can track more effectively the results of their marketing campaigns from the open rate to the conversion rate, in addition to how much money each campaign generates. Try to do the same with print, radio, banner, or even TV ads! Unless there's a telephone number embedded in your commercials and people are willing to share with you how they found your business, it's hard to track results and tweak your ads.

As a rule of thumb, you can expect to make $1 per lead and per offer that you send out. The bigger your list, the more money you will make. Besides that, you can segment your list into different groups, allowing you to better target your message and yield higher returns. You can connect with your audience through personalized messages about you, your business, and personal experiences. Educate them by giving out information people can use in their businesses or in their daily lives, which you should do by all means if you can rather than simply pushing offer after offer all day long.

The money is in the list; it's the motto in Internet marketing. Having an email list is the basis for building a foundation and a source of income on the Internet. Unlike interruption marketing, permission based marketing is also a two-way street because you can reply to messages sent to you unless the email newsletter you're subscribed to has a "no-reply" function. I have received answers to inquisitive questions I had in the past related to product launches, or to general questions most of the time.

Engagement Marketing

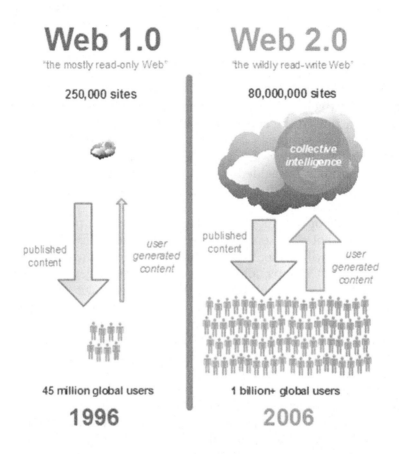

Fig. 1.15 Web 1.0 vs. Web 2.0

When the Internet started two decades ago, it was made up of links and websites allowing little or no interaction between users and businesses. With the rise of the blogosphere and social networking sites, the Web evolved from a space linking websites to one another to a space linking people to one another. It became a social gathering event where people were in front and center, sharing user generated content across the board. This process allowed businesses to connect much easier with customers subtly and in a non-intrusive fashion on multiple levels and have a meaningful exchange.

Social Buttons

Engagement marketing is permission-based marketing on steroids extended to social media; it's the next level. It is characterized by multifaceted interaction, allowing buyers and sellers to have fruitful exchanges, which result into a sale. Subscription happens in the form of "liking" your page, by "following" others, or by subscribing to your channel. Content sharing is the key, this fosters dialogue. Unlike permission marketing, the seller is not pushing offer after offer like he's capable of doing with email marketing, but is engaged in a constructive dialog with the buyer, where he tries to build trust and authority first and foremost.

Just like permission marketing, you get to talk to people who opted in to receive updates, but unlike permission marketing, engagement marketing allows you to refer others to products and services through word of mouth advertising.

Like *George Benckenstein* puts it, "The digital space is about engaging in a conversation with peers, customers and staff, innovating with them and constantly improving your value proposition in an authentic way." Customers have the power, the information, the advice and the resources to make their own decisions. In the digital world, it's about entering the conversation... It's about transparency and allowing consumers to participate and shape your brand based on authentic interactions between your employees, product or service, and your customers. It also turns the traditional marketing paradigm on its head — using the interaction with one to spread "affect and influence" through their personal network. He adds further: "It's about becoming involved. It's about shaping the future experiences you deliver to your customers. It's about human connection and relationships. Again — it is not a manufactured identity of the traditional brand." (Source: benckenstein.com)

Crystallizing the conversation to a point where the purchase becomes evident on social media is a daunting task not many businesses have mastered yet, either for lack of time and knowledge, or for applying the same old stiff corporate methods as mentioned above that worked once (which you cannot duplicate in this kind of environment).

The question becomes: How do you improve your value proposition in an authentic way? First, you show that you understand the problem and propose ways you can solve it. Communication is key! Secondly, relate your product or service to the source of the problem and delineate how it will improve their lives — which is what the buyer is looking for. You will make sales once you've demonstrated that A) you have the knowledge and understanding and B) you have the skill set needed to transform the buyer's life. In this paradigm you want to be more of a problem solver rather than a salesperson.

After creating that initial trust and authority, engagement marketing allows you to build customer loyalty. Nurturing relationships and showing appreciation towards your customers' business elicit customer loyalty. It's a way of following up by giving them a reason to want to participate more in your business. You begin with thank you and follow up messages, just to show them you care after the initial introduction. Your no. 1 goal is to give them a memorable experience they will want to repeat, and to make your customers feel special. The more special your customers feel, the more valuable they become and as a result, they will continue to buy and send you referrals.

Why do your current clients use your services? Is it purely geography; is it price, customer service or because people feel valued? Maybe your shop is fun and creative, you are really flexible, or you provide really great products and services. You need to dig deeper and find out what really motivates people to visit your shop and then give them that little extra push to stay with you. You can learn this information basically by asking questions. You can demonstrate what makes you and your business unique by showing them that you are a good caretaker with ongoing support and education in the form of newsletters, tips, advice, etc. You can demonstrate your creativity by creating fun and memorable campaigns they will take part in on your Facebook fan page, or on other venues. In this exercise, you are welcome to utilize more than just one method.

42

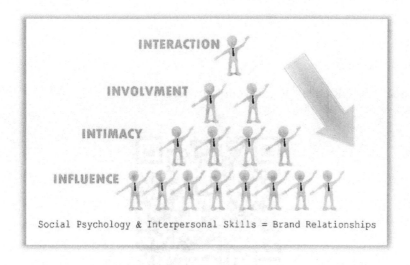

Fig. 1.16 Social Psychology and Interpersonal Skills = Brand Relationships

Scan this QR code[12] to test your knowledge:

---

[12] URL : https://goo.gl/jbakw8

Engaging Clients with Social Media

The *"80/20 Principle"* by British author and entrepreneur, Richard Koch, says that 80% of your profits are generated by 20% of your activities. In this book, Koch pioneered the idea that we can achieve more by working less, and enjoy life more by concentrating on the few things that matter uniquely to each aspect of our lives and by leaving 80% of the trivial things we do every day out of our focus.

The 80/20 ratio, also known as the Pareto Law, is a force of nature that explains why 20% of the people in any nation around the world possess 80% of the wealth and the land, why 80% of what we produce is generated during 20% of our working hours, why 20% of the clothes and shoes we buy are worn 80% of the time, why 80% of our personal telephone calls are to 20% of the people in our address book, why 20% of beer drinkers drink 80% of the beer, why 80% of your success comes from 20% of your efforts, why 80% of your innovation comes from 20% of your employees or customers, and why 80% of your income stream comes from 20% of your customers or activities. Following this school of thought, you should identify the 20% of the most productive and engaging clients in your business and build a strong relationship with them on social media.

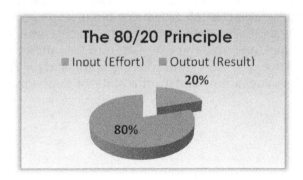

Fig. 1.17 The 80/20 Rule

You can gain and convert real customers, with the little example I gave on page 28 of the 50-100 active users who are spreading your messages across the board, instead of chasing 20,000 who either lack the time or interest for your business. When you start engaging people on social media, you usually don't have a list of followers to work with; most businesses don't have Facebook fan pages and Twitter accounts set up. If that's your case, you need to invite them on your business fan page or research where your target audience is online by utilizing 2 quick and easy sites: Google and Quantcast. If you don't have a fan page, you need to set one up. Typically, you need both a Facebook and Twitter account set up to run your business from a mobile app. You will need these 2 accounts integrated in your app to run your daily social media campaigns from your mobile business app. You need to engage those followers in a way that is meaningful and fun, as stated above, and virally spread your message using software and Facebook applications. Software applications for Facebook marketing are not particularly necessary but they help you achieve results much faster.

Who is your target audience and where can you find them? You are initially looking for people actively engaged in one way or the other on the Internet and who are passionate about your business or the industry you operate in. Let's say, for example, you run a wine shop and you'd like to connect with wine connoisseurs in your local area on your app so that they can frequent your business regularly. Where would you find them? You should locate people who are passionate about wine and who chat regularly about it... how about wine forums, for a start? Next, you'd research forums or blogs related to your industry on Google with active members — in this case, wines — and you'd pick one link you can plug into Quantcast, which is an intelligence website to find demographic stats such as the age, gender, education, and traffic stats of your target audience.

Fig. 1.18 Your Target Audience

In the graph[13] below, we can see that our target audience are U.S. females, aged 45-54 with no kids, an average income of $150K/year, graduated from school and have a college degree, and are Caucasian or don't belong to the African American, Asian, or Hispanic ethnic groups.

---

[13] http://www.winepress.us/forums

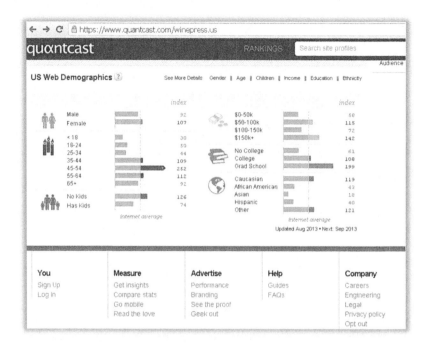

Fig. 1.19 Quantcast Search

Following this information, this is the group we shall target primarily on Facebook to grow our fan base and engage with on our business fan page. You need not spend all your money at once in an effort to grow your audience from 0 to 10K in one campaign, because you need just a few followers initially to get the ball rolling.

Aim for 100-300 and work your way upwards by growing your fan base organically and virally. A budget of $100-$200 will get you started and from thereon, you can move on to posting viral pictures and motivational quotes people will share like crazy on your fan page, or use whatever content you choose to go with.

Fig. 1.20 Viral Images and Quotes

There are many ways of landing clients in your business on Facebook fan pages. You do it with status updates, by running sidebar ads, promoted posts and with custom tabs on your Facebook fan page. You can also post links inside the description box in the *"About Us"* section, or you can collect them with Facebook referrals, in the form of shares and likes. Following the Pareto principal, we've identified 2 major places that convert more customers on your Facebook fan page than any other marketing tool. These are your status updates and your custom tabs.

Status updates is obvious because this is how you keep your page and your customers updated with new content and links to products and services; and custom tabs because that's where you convert that traffic with landing pages and other marketing tools used to collect more data and the names and email addresses of your customers. When you know this information, you can cut out 80% of the trivial activity that isn't working in your marketing campaigns and only concentrate on what's working to make more sales and generate new leads.

Fig. 1.21 Status Updates and Custom Tabs

Setting up Facebook ad campaigns to get "Likes" is not complicated. The process does not require a big learning curve; it's intuitive, seamless, and self-explanatory when you follow the steps. First, you need to click on the "Promote Page" button on the top right side of your fan page.

Promote Page

A **"Get More Page Likes"** window pops up in the browser and then you need to click on the little black gear symbol at the bottom left of the pop up window and then select the *"Advanced options"* option in the menu.

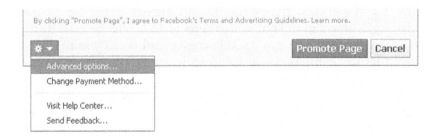

Get More Page Likes

Advanced Options

An **"Advertise on Facebook"** page will appear where you can set the parameters of your campaign. You can select the headline, text, landing view for your campaign, and fill in the information of your target audience, such as the location, age, interest, language, education, etc., in the *"Create Your Audience"* section of the form.

Get More Page Likes

In our wine connoisseur example, we would use the demographic information of our 45-54 year old U.S. females and target the city we live in. Last but not least, you'd set a daily budget you can afford for your ad campaign in the *"Campaign, Pricing, and Schedule"* in the last section of the form. In the headline box, you could put something like **"I love Apps,"** or whatever your page is about and in the text box, something like **"Click 'like' if you love apps,"** or whatever your page is about and you can change the default picture of the ad by uploading a new one. That's all there is to it. There's nothing fancy about it, this is not rocket science and when you're done, you'd let the campaign run for a while and you're ready to engage your first customers.

Once your page begins to populate, you will see who the most active members of your page are and ideally, you want to put them in a separate folder where you will manage them with great care. First, you'd post updates and share comments just to test their initial reaction and start engaging them. Social media is very effective when sharing relevant content that caters to your audience. Knowing what content — be it text, links, videos, or images — strikes a chord within your followers is a subtle balancing act, one that requires ongoing testing followed by fine tunings to filter out the exact formula needed to engage customers, convert, and grow your fan page virally. There's no rule that fits everything when it comes to Facebook and social media marketing because no two fan pages look or work the same. You need to test and tweak, refine and see what works in your marketing, then rinse and repeat until you finally grow your audience to the number you want. Having said that, pictures and quotes get more attention and tend to be shared faster than any other form of content you'll post on Facebook.

Knowing how to start your page is important. Knowing how to grow your fan base organically is equally important and adding some software to the mix to speed up the process can only benefit you. Also, knowing how to leverage Facebook and when to take advantage of its viral features is essential. You don't want to come late nor too early. You want to hit that share/send button when traffic is at its peak essentially, and before the beer foam formally dries out, so to speak.

Facebook uses an algorithm called "Edge rank," which takes several factors into account to make your content go viral and show up in other people's feeds. These factors are the affinity of your content, the weight, and time decay. The affinity, for example, is how appealing your content is to the user — if it caters to your follower's interests, etc. The weight speaks more to the type of engagement your content receives (i.e., more shares, comments, re-tweets, likes, etc.), and time decay is when the content was posted. Ideally, the best times to post are 7 AM, 5 PM, and 11 PM EST, before and after work and sometimes, before going to bed; and 9 PM-11 PM EST for the 18-24 demographic. For more information on the topic, please visit the following URL: http://www.whatisedgerank.com/

Facebook Edge rank

$$*\Sigma = U_e \; W_e \; D_e$$ (Ue=Affinity, We=Weight and De=Time decay)

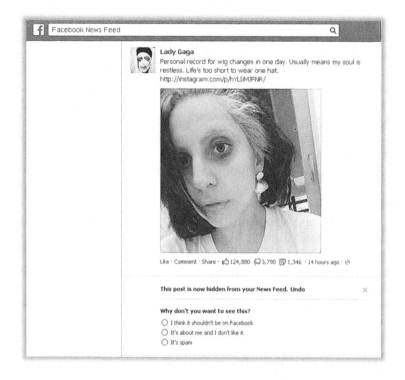

Fig. 1.22 Facebook News Feed

You can grow a list of followers on Twitter using software or by using websites that help you find potential clients in your target area. These software applications are *Tweet Adder* and *Hummingbird.* There are many others, but these are the ones commonly known.

Tweet Adder

They are auto-following marketing tools that make getting followers very easy, and you can follow up to 1,000 followers a day with just 2 minutes of work with these push-button software solutions. You can automate following, flawlessly unfollow people, and create a protected VIP list with both applications. The tools allow you to follow people based on location, keywords found in people's bios, tweets and hashtags, on competitors and people users are following. There are no ad costs associated in finding and following these potential clients; you just need to follow people and wait until they follow you back.

Having a large Twitter audience is not what's going to cut it in your marketing, however. You need to have a good strategy and know where your target audience is and follow them. Hummingbird retails for $69 with unlimited profiles and Tweet Adder will cost somewhere between $55 and $188, depending on the number of profiles you have. Other free tools you can work with to manage your list are *Twellow.com, Twitterlocal.net, Hashtags.org*, etc.

Twellow.com works like the Yellow Pages for Twitter and the website allows you to follow users you can start a conversation with based on keywords, location, and categories. Twitterlocal.net enables you to narrow down/filter Tweets coming from specific places. For example, you can put in a location like Buffalo, NY, in the search box, give it the range it needs to narrow down the search (i.e., 5, 10 miles or however many miles you want) and whoever is tweeting from those areas will show up on the feed. You'll be able to see what's going on and start a conversation. This could be relevant for any sort of local news or if you're just trying to find Twitter users in your local area.

Twitterlocal.net

Hashtags.org enables you to categorize your tweets so people can find them and understand what they're all about. Hashtags are always denoted first with a pound sign (#) and then with a certain keyword or phrase, example: "#Restaurant," "#Realestate," "#Chevrolet," "#ParisHilton," etc. Another great tool that was decommissioned lately is Twollow.com. This service is used to auto-follow users based on keywords found in tweets. Let's say, for example, you're selling a book called eBay 123 that teaches how to sell on eBay, and someone tweets about your book on Twitter. Twollow.com would automatically follow that person and add them onto your list. What a great way of following people seamlessly and effortlessly without needing to search for them!

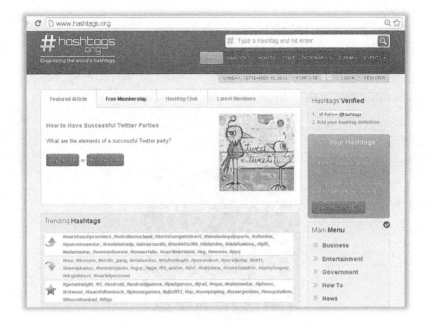

Hashtags.org

This is one aspect of social media marketing; there are many others you can use in your marketing than we have the time and space to cover in this book. If you search well, you can find good training programs and tutorials on how to sell using social media but with these tools alone, you have more than enough to get started. Basically, this is how viral marketing on Facebook and Twitter works, and it is not uncommon to grow a list of 10,000 followers on Facebook and Twitter in months with these tools and software applications.

A combination of software and a good strategy can grow your fan base exponentially on Facebook and Twitter, giving you a fair market read of your customer base and landing you good paying clients. Engagement marketing is for real, it is not a joke or a pastime for bored Facebook teenagers, but a real business model; one that works, one you can bank on to make repeat sales and serious money with your app, and one used to build businesses from scratch even in the worst economic environment imaginable, as we shall see in the next chapters.

Scan this QR code[14] to answer the second quiz:

Customer Retention

Customer attrition rate can be as high as 50% with no retention strategy in place and companies that boost customer loyalty campaigns by a minimum of 5% see an increase in revenue anywhere between 5-95%. So a small effort makes a huge difference because your customer feels special.

The common strategies people implement to retain customers are: one-time offers, customer rewards programs, and incentivized surveys. The problem with one-time offers is that you don't know if customers will come back, and for anyone who's done business with Groupon for example, you know what I'm talking about. Groupon is based precisely on this model and is nothing less but hope marketing. You sell your products and services for cheap, hoping to get some traction, but not knowing if you'll get repeat sales. Groupon offers customers a 50% discount that cuts out most of your profits just to try out your products and services. This is a great opportunity to get discovered by a new audience for a start-up, but how sustainable is this type of marketing really; how long can you stay in business when profits are skimmed off upfront just to attract customers in a very big way? Stories of businesses that went bust over this type of lead generation system are legendary. This is what Groupon's business model is all about.

Groupon

With customer rewards programs, you give customers some sort of financial compensation to incentivize people to purchase with you. The premise of incentivized surveys is to find out what people are looking for, and the best thing to do this is to reward them with future credits or financial compensation. These are fine methods, however, the problem is that people

59

are used to them and kind of expect them. An alternative to these methods is to create some direct rapport with clients, and ways to do this would be:

1. Build a list of key "VIPs" and nurture them
2. Create Customer Appreciation Days for your business
3. Events

As we've seen in the chapter before, when you build rapport and show your customers that you care, nothing is more rewarding to them than that. You could send them a handwritten quarterly note, for example, or do one once a year, or whatever you choose, and keep them updated with what you're doing. When you do this, they are filled with trust, it's such a boost for them and they are very appreciative.

With Customer Appreciation Days, you could open up your business to new customers by showing them how it works and you could stage events for product launches, promotions, and referrals to increase your brand awareness and get some media coverage. But how do you keep your customer happy and loyal? This is where most businesses fail.

Traditional businesses rely on used methods such as calling customers or sending postcards, letters, etc., for making repeat sales, which are time intensive and often don't yield the required results. Most businesses are happy when they land new customers, but often don't know when they'll come back, so what can they do? Most startups with the hottest products on the market will fall flat with no lead generation system in place to garner revenues. You could provide outstanding services, which most businesses in your neighborhood know how to do, but without a sound marketing system in place, you will not sell. Conversely, a business with a competent sales force to back up production will make money despite the fact that their products or services are mediocre. Most businesses will experience roller coaster growths with huge spikes followed by stiff drops; go from feast to hunger month in month out without a systematic lead generation strategy in place. According to the small business report 2018, 88% of business owners report that they consistently struggle with cash-flow. What's the difference between them and the 12% who do not have cash-flow problems? The 12% have systems in place that consistently bring in new prospects, appointments, and clients.

This is precisely where a business app and an email list come in pretty handy. Your mobile app provides you with the ability to build an email list you can use to nurture this relationship. An email list is essential for your business because you can manage and retain this client, no matter what. You will have a strategic advantage over your competition if you're using this kind of service because 95% of the time, most businesses don't do it. They don't know the value of email lists and how to exploit them. Most of them don't know this is how they can retain customers 99.9% of the time instead of making random phone calls and sending out post cards with dismal results.

Email auto-responders have been in usage for eons by online marketers; this is how they make sales and money online, and their value shouldn't be underestimated. Calling customers and sending post cards can be exhaustive and challenging, but with an email auto-responder, you can leverage your time by sending your customers a sequence of email series you've set up once, for the duration of one year. This is how you work smarter, not harder, and this is what an app can do for you.

The way you capture your customers' email and contact information is either by filling in the form inside your app you downloaded with a QR code scan, or by using the opt-in page of your mobile website. You should set up an opt-in page on both your app and mobile website and reward people with a free gift, tips, and information about whatever you're selling if they subscribe to your email list. This is how you can manage clients' long term rapport with an email list.

Imagine the excitement of your customer after their first visit, when you thank him or her for coming by and give him or her a few tips on how to keep a white smile, preserve their manicure, hair, or exercising more, etc. You could follow up 2 days later with a new email just to say hello and wanting to know how they're doing. If you think that's nothing, think again... For your customer, this is big news! This is huge, and they will love it! They will see that you're not indifferent and that you care. They will sense you are different than the competition and take notice. You could wait another week or 3 days and tell them you wanted to check about their hair, teeth,

61

or whatever you're selling and let them know about a 35% discount you have for them if they check in next week. A couple of weeks later, you could send coupons to redeem when they refer a friend, who gets a 25% discount for their first purchase, etc. In fact, you could keep your customer in the loop with updates in the weeks, months and years to come with tips, information, and trends and throw in special offers and discounts as you see fit, growing and nurturing this relationship even more to make repeat sales over and over as you want and make sure you keep them coming back.

Sending these email sequences will keep you fresh in their mind, and next time they need a haircut or manicure, who do you think they're going to call? Certainly not your competition because you're in their space! This is a far cry from the traditional methods used for retaining customers. Then, use this list to leverage the viral nature of Facebook and social media to land even more clients and get referrals by sharing pictures, tweets, "likes," and so many other things. Businesses that use marketing automation to nurture prospects experience a 451% increase in qualified leads (Source: The Annuitas Group). Relevant emails drive 18 times more revenue than broadcast emails (Source: Jupiter Research) and nurtured leads make 47% larger purchases than non-nurtured leads (Source: The Annuitas Group). If you see the potential here, now you know how engagement marketing and email marketing really works.

"Hi Stacey, this is Dr. Scott"

How to Measure Your ROI

It's important to identify the right KPIs for your app depending on the niche market you operate in. Many KPIs are used to measure different functionalities of an app, relative to its effectiveness in terms of performance and interface usability. Your return on investment (ROI) using social media, as referred to in Chapter 3 will depend on these factors:

1. Your Content/Message
2. Level of Engagement & Conversion Rate
3. Product/Brand
4. App Downloads & Referrals

You can't put an exact figure on your social media's ROI because this is a case-by-case situation. Not all markets are the same and you need to see your social media activities and your app marketing as a long term investment, rather than a one-off quick sales opportunity. First off, define what success is and how you want to achieve it. Get a clear understanding about your goals, short term and long term and have measurable milestones with which you can steer your campaign in the right direction. If brand awareness and image management are your prime objectives, this requires a long-term commitment on your part because you need to grow and nurture your audience with content that increases your brand's equity and builds loyalty. Such content includes your product line, prices, market niche & size, competition, your growth projection, company's policy, your mission statement and goals, your corporate identity, etc. On the other hand, if your goal is to make sales, this can be achieved much quicker with targeted ad campaigns.

Key performance indicators or KPIs in short, are metrics by which you can measure how effective your app campaign is. This includes how often you are mentioned, the increase in website traffic, your client's feedback, reputation, your conversion rate, referrals, your lead generation, your app download, and many other things. The process of optimizing the KPIs will improve your revenue efficiency inside your app dramatically. The level of engagement will affect the conversion rate inside your app, which in turn is affected by the type of content you put out and how the client responds to it. Your product/catalog click-through rate is another major KPI subject to rigorous tweaking and testing in terms of its image layout, product description and interface usability. The overall product click-through rate is a mere reflection of the catalog layout. At this stage when sales are triggered on a daily basis, this signals that the engagement rate is at its optimal level.

What is your client worth, $250, $2,500, $50,000, $100,000, $1 Million, or more? If you know the value of your leads, you know what it takes to make a successful ROI. Twenty to 40 leads per day or per month is what you're looking at? You need to break down your sales figures into days and weeks and figure out how many leads this represents in terms of income and adjust your KPIs accordingly. Based on the information above, you need to crunch the numbers and set benchmarks that will steer you towards your desired goal. Which KPI affects sales in your business? You need to know this up front so you can spend more time and energy tweaking it every day to meet your set goals or surpass them. You need to know what message converts best and tweak it even further or work on your product click-through rate, app downloads, etc. However, given the market, bear in mind that any lead you land may not necessarily convert into a sale the minute they join your list. If these are fresh leads, it takes some time before they are acquainted to your business and in most cases, they'll respond after the 7th email they receive. This is an average seen in Internet marketing. Throwing in discounts and special offers is one way to drag them much faster to your shop and on a regular basis. In fact, the first sequence of emails should always include one-off special offers, tips, how to information, or anything else that's related to your industry so that you can build one-on-one rapports and get them used to your business.

In the long run, you will make money and recoup your initial investment! You also must know what motivated followers to like your Facebook fan page.

Forty percent of the people surveyed said they like to receive discounts and promotions, 39% to show support for the company to others, 36% to get a "freebie" (e.g., free samples, coupon), 34% to stay informed about the activities of a company, 33% to get updates on future products, 30% to get updates on upcoming sales, 29% for fun or entertainment, 25% to get access to exclusive content, 22% were referred by someone, 21% to learn more about the company, 13% for education about company topics, 13% to interact (e.g., share ideas, provide feedback). (Source: Buddy Media) Obviously, discount and promotion followers are where the money is on Facebook; you should give preferential treatment to this information.

Former Melrose Jewelers now Melrose.com, LLC, a L.A. jewelry and watch retailer founded in 2008 by USC MBA graduate Krishan Agarwal, and that ships on 4 continents worldwide, is a leading example of a successful ROI implementation using social media. The company sells high-end watches like Rolex and Breitling, where the average sale is $5,000. They offered consumers $100 off in their first promotions on their next purchase if they "Liked" them on Facebook.

They had an app on their Facebook fan page, which functioned as a simple quiz where, after taking the quiz, your "watch personality" was revealed at the end (e.g., you are James Bond, 2000 Breitling man, etc.) to engage and secure email addresses of potential customers. You also received $150 off after your purchase if you took a picture of your new watch and posted it on Facebook, which was meant to kick start their Facebook viral campaign! As a result, Facebook fans went from 30,000 to over 180,000 (600% increase) in one quarter because of viral traffic, and sales went from a few hundred thousand to over $2,000,000.[15]

---

[15] Source: http://www.slideshare.net/91654/166-case-studies

Melrose.com Facebook[16] fan page:

Booshaka.com and *Twittersearch.com* are 2 practical applications used to track the most engaging followers on Facebook and Twitter so you can spend more time talking to them and get the most bangs for your buck. It is known that 10% of the community drives most of the conversation on social media, so you must pay attention to what they say and show your appreciation for their contribution. This application shows top fans, top posters, and top movers inside your fan base, and you will come to know who is or is not an easy sale, based on their responses.

---

[16] https://www.facebook.com/MelroseCom

Booshaka.com

The buzz and curiosity you create around your business and your app will definitely impact your sales and app downloads and this, in turn, will fuel your reach on social media.

Any time someone shares, post comments, re-tweets, or likes your fan page, their activity shows up in other feeds and those viral links and images, like in the Melrose example, will drive even more traffic to your business, your website, and your app. Each app downloaded once means A) a new lead for you and B) this new lead will push the boundaries of your reach even further and attract new customers in your sales funnel each time someone tweets, likes, and shares links about your business. This perpetual self-feeding cycle of viral traffic can only mean 3 things: more sales, a bigger reach, and ultimately a greater return on investment.

Social Media ROI Case Studies

In this segment, we are going to showcase successful ROI case studies using social media that you can learn from and see if they apply to your business. We shall begin with Joe Sorge and AJ Bombers, a burger restaurant in Milwaukee, Wisconsin.

Case Study #1: Joe Sorge Owner of AJ BOMBERS in Milwaukee, WI, USA

After six months of break-even sales and no money for traditional marketing, Joe Sorge, the owner of AJ Bombers, a burger restaurant in Milwaukee, started using Twitter to attract customers. Within a year, weekly sales increased +60% without spending $1 in traditional media! What happened? In a response he gave via Skype to a Rutgers' class at the State University in NJ, when asked why he started tweeting, Joe said, "I was scared. I opened a restaurant in Milwaukee at the worst time in the worst economy since the Great Depression. I sat at my computer wondering how I could make this work. When I found people on Twitter talking about my restaurant and my burgers, I jumped in." Good feedback from customers on Twitter helped build relationships and Twitter followers soon accounted for 75% of AJ Bomber's customers.

AJ Bombers now has 19,000+ Twitter followers, success with Foursquare, where he declared a "Foursquare Day" to earn a Swarn Badge, which increased sales +110%, a "Food Wars" episode on the Travel Channel and the sales to go with it. Not bad for a restaurant with two locations in Wisconsin.

Joe uses Twitter regularly for outreach and as an extra pair of eyes and ears to listen and respond to customers. Joe says he uses permission marketing, which means he won't talk to clients if they don't talk back, instead of traditional outbound marketing and says he's never spent a dime on outbound advertising and if he did, it wasn't more than $500 for the past 18 months since launching his Twitter campaign. He says interruption marketing is not as effective as permission marketing

69

and this is why he's not a staunch supporter of this type of marketing.

Joe recently started a company called Kitchen Table Companies with a show on The Pulse Network with American author, journalist, and marketing consultant, Chris Brogan, who's also CEO and President of Human Business Works based in Portland, Maine, to help small businesses. You can learn more about Joe and AJ Bombers by scanning the QR codes below.

Video: http://youtu.be/ZpnNnLGmOBQ

Video: http://youtu.be/mDZ69oQe-uM

AJ BOMBERS[17], 1247 N Water Street Milwaukee, WI 53202

The second case study is a perfect example of the sheer power of social media when selling products and services to customers online. In this unique example, none of the customers were acquired through traditional advertising; all was done with a simple Facebook fan page and a Twitter account. Meet Mari Luangrath, owner of Foiled Cupcakes in Naperville, IL, who began her business connecting with customers with no traffic and no website.

Case Study #2: Mari Luangrath Owner at FOILED CUPCAKES in Naperville, IL, USA

Foiled Cupcakes, a Chicago company that bakes and sells cupcakes, has no store front, only a website and there's no way for consumers to experience their product before they buy unless they establish a relationship with them through social media! When the product was ready, but the launch of the website was delayed, they relied on Facebook and Twitter for CRM. Social media generated 93% of its business through social media leads to surpass revenue target by +600%.

The reason: You can tweet all day long; you can update your Facebook page all day long but are people listening? "They'll listen if they know you care about them! So my personal mandate is that I reply to every single tweet and make a comment on every single post to our Facebook page," says owner, Mari Luangrath. She also says, "We know every single one of our customers by name! We've probably had a good Twitter or Facebook conversation with them before they even call us." That's courageous customer relationship marketing, one that clearly shows you can run a business with tweets and Facebook posts.

---

[17] Website: http://ajbombers.com

Video: http://youtu.be/WxuSZklWCZI

Video: http://youtu.be/1h8K-_fHbOc

FOILED CUPCAKES[18], P.O. Box 2462, Naperville, IL 60567

Case Study #3: DOMINO'S PIZZA UK & IRELAND LTD

Our third case study Domino's Pizza in the UK has reported a 29% surge in pre-tax profits to £17.5m, buoyed by a strong performance from E-commerce sales and attributed its link-up with Foursquare as key to its recent performance.

---

[18] Website: http://www.foiledcupcakes.com

The takeaway company reported a like-for-like sales increase in 553 stores by 13.7% in the 26-week period to the end of 27 June 2010. Domino's now has 627 stores in the UK after 19 new stores were opened in the period. The company said it was on track for a further 55 store openings the same year.

The group — which celebrated 25 years of business — highlighted its E-commerce business as the stand-out performer. It said sales in its E-commerce unit had grown by 61.4% in the period and that online sales now accounted for 32.7% of overall UK delivered sales.

In May 2010, Domino's launched a nationwide promotion on Foursquare that encouraged users to check-in at its outlets. In 2010, Domino's financial results proved that it "led the way with social media initiatives such as affiliate marketing, our superfans programmes and the development of a link up with Foursquare, the location-based social media site." It added that its web-based activity had afforded it the dual benefit of "driving pizza sales" and "building customer loyalty."

Video: http://youtu.be/ZR5FNJDNwW0

DOMINO'S[19] PIZZA, 1 Thornbury, West Ashland, Milton Keynes MK6 4BB, UK.

---

[19] Website: http://www.dominos.co.uk

Case Study #4: EMERSON SALON in Seattle, WA, USA

If you're active on Facebook and Twitter, there is a fair chance you might have heard of Emerson Salon; the social savvy salon that has enjoyed great success through channels like Facebook, Twitter, and their blog.

An industry that depends heavily on word of mouth, Emerson Salon doesn't just sit and wait. It is actively building relationships and thought leadership through social media, accelerating the word of mouth effect. Stylists are also featured on the website homepage with extensive personal information to allow visitors to understand the stylist like a true friend. The success was so prominent that 75% of Emerson's customers are from Facebook, Twitter, and their blog. This built business because 90% of all purchase decision begins on the Internet and 85% are looking for an independent review.

Matt Buchan, co-founder of Emerson, commented, "It's rare for even a walk-in customer to come in and not have read our blog or seen our tweets." The buzz is loud for good reasons. On Yelp, comments are highly positive with 4 to 5 stars ratings. One review in 2010 was a mixture of great customer service and professional skills. Many small businesses provide excellent services but often receive unsatisfactory return mainly because of insufficient exposure. With limited budget, time and sweat are your greatest assets. Take a shot in social media they say, and see if it improves your business. But before that, conduct some quick and dirty research. Understand if your target audiences are on Facebook and Twitter first and craft a simple plan that best suits your busy schedule.

★★★★★ 6/4/2010

Kati S.
Seattle, WA

Emily is the BEST hair stylist I have ever had. She actually cares about each client as an individual. I have had her call me on numerous occasions and tell me she's scheduling an appointment because she has envisioned a cut for my hair specifically. Guess what? She's always right about what she envisioned and my hair always looks incredible. I literally don't even have to tell her what I want her to do because she knows my hair so well that I can sit in the chair and trust that whatever she does will be amazing.

She has always answered all my questions about hair care and cut/color and she explains all of the steps she goes through to make me look like a rock star by the end of the appointment. :)

My hair has never been healthier, nor has it ever been as stand out as when Emily has been in charge of my tresses. People constantly ask me if they can take a picture of my cut, where I get it cut and who does it. They also compliment on Emily impeccable use of color.

Emerson Salon is truly blessed to have Emily work with them. Go get your hair done by her and enjoy the ambiance as well as the other kick-ass people on staff. You'll never want to get your hair done elsewhere.

EMERSON SALON[20], 909 E Pike St, Seattle, WA 98122

Case Study #5: CISCO SYSTEMS, San Jose, CA, USA

The launch of a new router in 2008 using only social media would provide the proof Cisco's marketers were seeking to make the case for an exceptional ROI. The results surprised even the social media enthusiasts. With this single project, the company shaved six figures off its launch expenses and set a new precedent for future product launches. Up to that point, the traditional product launch went something like this:

- Fly in more than 100 executives and press members from 100 countries to headquarters in San Jose, California
- Take a few hours of the CEO's or an executive's time to prep and present

---

[20] Website: http://emersonsalon.com

- Distribute well-crafted, but static, press releases to key media
- Email customers
- Run print ads in major business newspapers and magazines

For its Aggregated Services Router (ASR) launch, Cisco aimed to execute entirely online leveraging social media, and in doing so, engage network engineers in a more interactive, fun way. Cisco met its audience where they were, in online venues and the gaming world. The company built a stage with big-screen monitors, chairs for the audience and palm trees for its flagship launch event entirely in a Second Life environment. It then piped in video of executives presenting the ASR.

More than 20,000 network engineers learned as they played a 3D game, wherein they "defended the network" using the ASR. Research shows that 17% to 18% of IT professionals play games online every day. Top scorers went on to a championship round with the winner, bagging $10,000 plus a router. Additionally, the company heavily used video to educate customers and the media about the ASR, encouraging them to pass along links via social sharing. Hardcore network engineers could connect on the Cisco Support Group for Uber User Internet Addicts on Facebook. "It allowed them to connect with Cisco in a new way, and build preference and customer loyalty," said LaSandra Brill, the senior manager of global social media at Cisco. The company's next-generation video conferencing technology brought customers together at local offices around the globe. Executives back in San Jose could see the audience's facial expressions and vice versa.

Cisco assembled videos, content, and images in a widget format and embedded it into "social media" news releases and launch pages. Bloggers and others could spread the information easily with the embedded code. A video datasheet engaged engineers on their mobile devices. Cisco seeded its Networking Professionals Technology Community Forum with launch-related discussion topics and gave customers an "Ask the Expert" function. The whole campaign spanned three months with the launch in the middle. During pre-launch,

launch, and post-launch, Cisco kept the audience engaged by encouraging discussion with and among its audience.

Compared to traditional launches of the past, the ASR launch delivered eye-opening numbers. More than 9,000 people (90 times more than past launches) from 128 countries attended virtual launch events. Without travel, the launch saved an estimated 42,000 gallons of gas. Print ads were largely replaced with media coverage, including nearly three times as many press articles as a comparable traditional launch, more than 1,000 blog posts and 40 million online impressions. Plus, top executives spent only about an hour recording the video presentation. The whole launch cost one-sixth of a similar launch that used traditional outreach methods.

The ASR launch effectively tore the lid off social media at Cisco, which now truly walks its talk regarding the power of networks. Since then, social networking comes standard with every product launch and print advertising funds have largely moved to social activities. And media like video, Facebook, and Twitter keep customers and the press engaged continuously. With subsequent launches, the company has realized even greater ROI — now seeing costs just one-seventh of those before. But the networking company keeps pursuing even greater returns with social networking.

"Now that we've got that buy-in, we need to just continue to show the success of one campaign over another," Brill said. Tools like Radian6 and Symphony help the core social media team, now eight people measure the impact relative to cost of each campaign. After every campaign, the team just sets new benchmarks to beat. "Social media doesn't replace the need for white papers or sales interaction. I think it helps accelerate and shorten the sales cycle," Brill said. "There are studies out there that people who are involved in communities and engaged with the brand are likely to spend up to 50% more than those who are not. We want to try to prove that." (Source: socialmediaexaminer.com)

CISCO SYSTEMS[21], 170 West Tasman Dr. San Jose, CA 95134

---

[21] Website: http://www.cisco.com

This next case study illustrates how customer retention works using social media. It's been proven that it takes twice the energy to land new clients than it takes to retain old ones. In this example, we are going to show why engaging customers is utterly vital not only to make sales, but to also build loyalty.

Case Study #6: JETBLUE AIRWAYS, Long Island City, NY, USA

This is the story of Dave Raffaele, a blogger and Twitter user who was flying with JetBlue (@jetblue) on 2 occasions and how he used Twitter to enhance his customer experience and address concerns in real time. This example sheds more light on the power of Twitter and social media than any white paper or elevator pitch ever could and here's what we learned about his experience with the airline carrier:

"This is how JetBlue, and the people on Twitter, used Social Media to treat me like a human:"

Leg #1 – Boston to Denver

I was taking JetBlue for the first time on a 2 day business trip to Denver. On the flight out I think someone accidentally hit the thermostat with their carry-on because I swear it was a minimum of 80 degrees on the plane. When I arrived, feeling even filthier than I usually do when getting off of a 4.5 hour flight, I decided to shoot this tweet to JetBlue and let them in on my discomfort.

@jetblue...you Need to turn down the heat on your 7:55pm flight from Boston to Den ver. It was rough.

12:32 AM Dec 15th, 2008 from Twittelator in reply to JetBlue

 JetBlue Thanks for the heads up! (sometimes flight crews get overzealous traveling from cold to cold!) *12:34 AM Dec 15th, 2008*

In less than 2 minutes, JetBlue responded with this tweet acknowledging my concern. It may seem like a small thing, but think about it. Here is a huge organization listening to me complain about the temperature on their plane over a channel that is far from mainstream. Even more impressive is that it was not an automated response. There was a real person writing that little note. It may not sell more plane tickets, but it definitely made me tell this story.

Leg #2 – Denver to Boston

Now it was time for the return flight home and this time it was a red-eye. I was already grumpy about having to try and sleep in a seat designed for a 10 year old child, so I decided to get there a few hours early, relax, and do some reading. I used one of the kiosks to check in and headed up to the counter to check in my bag. Low and behold, there was no one at the counter. It was a ghost town. My plan was shot. Perturbed with my iPhone in hand, I turned to Twitter and shot this tweet over the bow of my new friends at JetBlue:

@jetblue In denver and want to check my bag but there us no one at the counter. What's wrong with this picture?

10:39 PM Dec 16th, 2008 from Twittelator in reply to JetBlue

sogrady: @daveraffaele: the JetBlue crew in Denver's usually only there ~2 hrs before the flight. you'll probably have to wait 30-45 minutes.
about 1 month ago · Reply · View Tweet · Show Conversation

JetBlue @sogrady is a step ahead of me – but sending a note to the GM and Supes as a heads up anyway. Are there many waiting? *10:46 PM Dec 16th, 2008*

daveraffaele: @JetBlue There are probably 5 or 6 people waiting. Not too bad
about 1 month ago · Reply · View Tweet · Show Conversation

JetBlue sent a note to Theresa our General Manager out there *11:08 PM Dec 16th, 2008*

JetBlue you should see some Crewmembers showing up shortly – our offices in DEN are away from the ticket counter. *11:15 PM Dec 16th, 2008*

daveraffaele: @JetBlue, @sogrady Thanks for the tag team action. @michellebb and I will just hang out in Hudson news for a while. :)
about 1 month ago · Reply · View Tweet · Show Conversation

Not only did JetBlue respond to me directly, but other folks who follow me on Twitter also gave me insight based on their own experience. JetBlue, with the help of the crowd, was again able to turn a situation that would have normally annoyed me into one of understanding and outstanding customer experience. JetBlue gets it and Twitter helped them deliver it. Just awesome! (Source: daveraffaele.com)

JETBLUE AIRWAYS[22], 27-01 Queens Plaza N, Long Island City, NY 11101

(Source: http://www.slideshare.net/91654/166-case-studies)

As we've seen in these examples, 2 businesses were able to take off and break even in a short period of time with no website; just one Twitter and Facebook account. One company increased sales by 29% nationwide with Foursquare. Another generated 75% of its leads through relationship building and savvy word-of-mouth advertising. A third one was able to slash advertising costs down to a fraction of what it used to spend, and a fourth was able to retain customers by addressing concerns in real time, proving that social media is not a fad, but a real business model for repeat sales and customer retention.

In the example of AJ Bombers, Joe Sorge spent $500 total on outbound advertising since he first started his Twitter campaign, proving that engagement marketing works and that it outperforms interruption marketing with 60% increase in sales. This shows that you don't have to spend money to make money, and proves how much power you can gain when social media is used in conjunction with a mobile app that's ready for download in the app stores.

---

[22] Website: http://www.jetblue.com

How SMS Text Marketing Works

Mobile is the fastest growing industry on the planet. Take every type of PC around the world, including desktops, laptops, netbooks and tablet PCs, add them together, and we have 1.5 billion in use worldwide. However, mobile is nearly 5 times larger. There are 2 billion TV sets in use globally, but mobile has 3.5 times more users. Worldwide, there are 1.1 billion landline phones; yet mobile is larger with 7.1 billion mobile subscriptions, which is more than six times bigger.

The 7.1 billion mobile subscriptions are not "unique users" and are "handsets in use." The number of unique users is now 4.5 billion, or 63% of all the humans alive on the Earth. The remaining 2.6 billion accounts are second or third accounts for the same user. The number of phones in use is estimated at 5.4 billion mobile handsets around the world. Out of the 4.5 billion unique user number, 900 million carry two phones, meaning 20%, or one in five who have a mobile subscription or account, actually walks around with two phones (Source: TomiAhonen Almanac 2014).

According to Boston Consulting Group, mobile usage jumped to $3.3 trillion high in sales in 2014, doubling the sales from its total of $1.56 trillion in sales in 2013. In 2010 the value of the mobile reached $1.18 trillion. That was an increase of 9% from the year before and in 2012 it grossed $1.45 trillion in sales (Source: TomiAhonen Almanac 2013). The growth rate had been an average annual 7-9% prior to the huge spike in 2014.

The $1.56 trillion in sales in 2013 breaks down into 1.15 trillion service revenues, such as phone calls, messages, Internet access, music, games, advertising, apps, etc. The $280 billion were spent on handset sales, mostly Smartphones, and another $125 billion in hardware that includes a wide range of products from networking equipment to accessories.

81

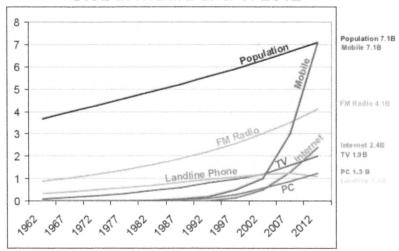

Fig. 1.23[23] Global Media End of 2012

The mobile operators/carriers still make up the majority of the revenues with voice calls and messaging. Voice calls were worth $673 billion in sales, while messaging was worth $199 billion in sales. Of that, SMS text messaging was worth $130 billion in sales in 2013 and MMS brought in another $46 billion.

Industry's Highest Open Rate
Ninety-seven percent of all text messages are read within four minutes of being sent against only 16% for emails. With figures like that, it's rare that your message won't get opened up by potential customers. SMS text messages allow you to send advertisements to your target audience as often as you want with special offers and discounts.

This service is the equivalent of having a line of people outside your store, waiting for the right opportunity to make a purchase. Print, radio or TV requires a substantial investment

---

[23] Source: TomiAhonen Almanac 2012 & TomiAhonen Forecast 2012-2015

prior to generating sales. The cost of mobile marketing, however, pales in comparison and the effects are felt almost instantly. Not only does SMS marketing put your product and service in front of the right audience, but it also builds a long-lasting loyal customer base for your business. The longer you stay in the loop, the stronger your presence is being felt.

The reason it enjoys such a high open rate is because SMS marketing is permission-based marketing on steroids. You can't help but open the message when you hear that little buzz in your pocket. It's instinctive, intuitive and comes close to being an addiction. There is no spam or invasion of privacy issues because people opted in to receive your messages just like with email marketing.

SMS stands for "short message service." It is text messaging over a cell phone and with MMS, which stands for "multimedia messaging service" you can send images, voice, videos, or some combination of these message types along with text. Each message sent is highly targeted specifically to those looking for your services. And with response rates ranging from 10 to 70 out of every 100 texts, compare that to the 1.5 to 3% response rate for most other types of advertising, and you can bet your business will grow as a result. So how does it work?

1st) Your customer opts into your list by texting a special keyword like text "FREEPIZZA" to 313131 to get a free pizza.

2nd) Your customer receives an automated message or special offer promoting your services.

Fig. 1.24 "Text Deals to 727272"

Here are some of the things an SMS advertising campaign can do for your business:

1. Just like in email marketing, you can build a list of potential buyers who are segmented according to democratic scenarios of interest. The analytics that come with mobile show preferences profiled on buying patterns. They can make each marketing campaign more targeted than the last and increase the response rate in sales. They can also be used to make other marketing channels more profitable.

2. You can create an alert list for specials for people who have told you what they're interested in. You can send an alert out in less than five minutes and see an immediate response.

3. You can send mobile coupons to have point-of-sale redemption. Mobile coupons are less expensive than traditional coupons in that there is no design, printing or mailing costs. Because a coupon resides on the person's phone, there is less of a chance it will get lost and more of a chance it'll drive foot traffic to your store.

4. You can do location-based campaigns. How would you like to be able to broadcast the specials you have to the people who've opted in to receive messages from you when the person is within a certain radius of your store? You can send geo-fence messages, which allows you to target multiple specific geographic areas even down to the zip code or server mount radius from your stores. Not only do you save money by not sending messages out to people who are not likely to respond, but you can also send different offers for each geographical area. One of the problems with many other forms of advertising is that it's hard to measure where the sale came from. If you only knew how, you could eliminate the ads that are not working and put more money on those that do work. You could turn traditional advertising mediums into immeasurable direct response campaigns.

SMS ROI Case Studies

In this chapter we are going to showcase examples of successful ROI using SMS text campaigns and we shall begin with the Clearwater-based Hooters Restaurant chain in Florida.

Case Study #1: HOOTERS RESTAURANTS, Clearwater, FL, USA

"Hooters sweepstakes beefs up mobile database."

A couple of years ago, the Hooters Restaurant chain used a contest involving people's mobile phones to help launch their national promotion to build up the Hooters Mobile Club, which at the time had more than 50,000 members. Thousands of customers followed the advice of the in-store signage to text "POOL" to enter to win a trip to the Hooters Super Pool Party in Miami's South Beach. "Using mobile platforms proved to be a very efficient way to run our national contest and was a more effective way to collect customers' information," said Noela Scarano, director of marketing for Hooters of America Inc., Atlanta. "We were very pleased with the results."

Hooters is well-known for its brand of food and fun, featuring a casual beach-theme atmosphere, a menu that features seafood, sandwiches and Hooters' nearly world-famous chicken wings, and service provided by the All-American cheerleaders, the Hooters Girls. The contest was used as an incentive to join the Hooters Mobile Club. All entrants are now signed up for getting periodic offers such as mobile coupons, event alerts and other discounts. This has given Hooters the ability to remarket to those consumers, which is an important part of the company's overall marketing strategy. The Hooters Mobile Club now has over 50,000 members.

How the Contest Worked

For 10 days Hooters took over the pool at the Surfcomber Hotel and gave customers a chance to be at the epicenter of fun in South Beach. They chose five lucky grand prize winners from the eligible entries to attend a party at the Surfcomber Hotel in Jan and Feb of 2010. The Hooters Pool Party was complete with bikini clad Hooters Girls, giveaways, and live music, including a performance by Uncle Kracker and DJ Skribble.

Hooters also wanted to target football fans and customers who wanted to share in the brand. The Pro Bowl and the Super Bowl were also played in Miami during the week of the party, so it seemed like a natural fit. "Hooters chose mobile as the primary method of entry because customers could instantly sign up while they were still in the store," said Cindy Setlock, director of national accounts at [service provider]. "Mobile text doesn't require Internet access or paper," she said. "It allows Hooters to take part in a 'Go Green' initiative and communicate offers to mobile customers instantly and electronically."

Senior Editor Giselle Tsirulnik covers advertising, messaging, legal/privacy and database/CRM. Reach her at giselle@mobilemarketer.com. The original article is here: http://www.mobilemarketer.com/cms/news/messaging/5057.html.

HOOTERS RESTAURANTS[24], 107 Hampton Road Ste 200 Clearwater, FL 33759

Case Study #2: STARBUCKS, Seattle, WA, USA

When it comes to mobile, Starbucks is one of the companies that leads the pack, no matter what channel they are using. To promote its My Starbucks Rewards program, the company ran an in-store call to action. The call to action was positioned near the drink counter so when consumers waited for their drinks, they could text-in.

Coffee lovers were encouraged to text the keyword GOLD to the short code 697289 (MYSBUX). When consumers texted-in, they received a message from Starbucks that thanked them for their interest in the program. For this instance, SMS helped Starbucks build up its My Starbucks Rewards program. Additionally, but using the in-store call to action, the company was able to reach more consumers as they were waiting for their drink.

---

[24] Website: http://www.hooters.com

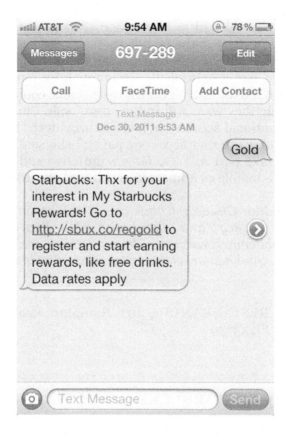

STARBUCKS[25], PO Box 3717, Seattle, WA 98124-3717

Case Study #3: COCA-COLA, Atlanta, GA, USA

Coca-Cola is no stranger to SMS and it was no surprise that the company was going to tap the channel when it came to promoting its latest initiative centered around March Madness.

Coca-Cola's Coke Zero ran an interactive SMS program that rewarded users with prizes when they watched March Madness games. The campaign centered around the 2012 NCAA Division I Men's Basketball Championship games and during the games, an SMS call-to-action was promoted with on-air

---

[25] http://www.starbucks.com

keywords and alerts with the Coke Zero logo that prompted users to text-in to win prizes. Additionally, consumers could find codes on March Madness-themed Coke Zero products and cups and text them to the short code 2653. The initiative was a great way to have users interact with their mobile device when they were watching a game at home.

THE COCA-COLA COMPANY[26], 1 Coca Cola Plz NW, Atlanta, GA 30313

Case Study #4: JCPENNEY, Plano, TX, USA

Department store JCPenney thought outside the box when it came to promoting its Easter dresses. The time-sensitive campaign centered around JCPenney sending out SMS messages to its opted in consumers to drive them in-store for a one-day event. Additionally, the SMS message included a link that allowed users shop for Easter clothing from the company's mobile site. This is a good example of a company that is using their current mobile database to reach its customers and drive

---

[26] http://www.coca-colacompany.com

sales. The one-day event was time-sensitive and SMS was a great channel to quickly get the word out about it.

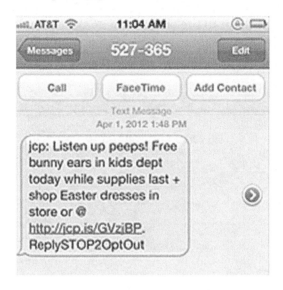

JCPENNEY[27], 6501 Legacy Drive Plano, Texas 75024

Case Study #5: RITE AID, Camp Hill, PA, USA

Rite Aid is another company that used SMS to help drive donations. To kick off its 18th annual Miracle Balloon campaign on April 1, 2010, benefiting Children's Miracle Network Hospitals, Rite Aid invited its shoppers to text the keyword RAKIDS to the short code 50555 and make a $5 donation.

Rite Aid proved that SMS can be used to drive awareness of a good cause and to get consumers involved. Additionally, instead of simply asking them for a donation at the point-of-sale, Rite Aid used SMS to have consumers make their own choice about the donation.

---

[27] http://www.jcpenney.com

RITE AID[28], PO Box 3165 Harrisburg, PA, 17105

These are interesting case studies with successful ROI campaigns; you can find more of these at these URLs:

http://www.mobilemarketer.com/cms/news/messaging/12
633.html

http://www.mobilemarketer.com/cms/news/messaging/13
280.html

---

[28] https://www.riteaid.com

SMS text marketing is a third party service operating outside of your app that can be utilized in conjunction with your app when pushing offers to customers. Your app allows you to send push-notifications that will achieve the same results as with SMS text messaging; I have added this extra information because you have the capability to create special offers, coupons and discounts inside your app. In the next section, we shall dive into the functionalities you can find inside a business app.

PART TWO: ANATOMY OF A BUSINESS APP

In this section, we briefly look at the basic functionalities you can find inside a business app. We show you how they can be used to manage sales and customers, and enhance the user experience.

Anticipating Markets

"End-users not technologies shape the market. Consequently marketers need to stay abreast not only of technological developments but also of the way people respond to them." – Matt Haig, author.

If you're a shop owner, run a business, or planning on selling products and services, pay close attention because this information is for you. Many people doubt the influence of mobile apps, especially those with small businesses. There is this miscomprehension that mobile apps are only effective in large businesses. In all actuality, the barrier to entering the mobile apps market is quite low, and very simple at that, irrespective of a business' size. In fact, mobile apps can be viewed as a determinant of demand because it is a variable that can influence demand and shift the demand curve in a positive direction, if utilized correctly. Adding to that, mobile apps can also be seen as a form of globalization in the business because they create an interconnectedness in many areas such as communication, people, knowledge and ideas to name a few, between consumer/seller and throughout the industry the business operates in. That being said, people should start to realize that mobile apps could certainly benefit small businesses as well.

Take a stroll around your neighborhood and take notice of the different businesses around you. Deliberate upon restaurants that can use a mobile app to allow pre-orders, allowing customers to order and pay for their meals through the app and have their food at the table as soon as they arrive at the restaurant. Think of supermarkets that can use mobile apps and utilize push-notifications to notify consumers about special offers and food clearance sales. Consider bookshops that may use a mobile app to promote new books, student discounts and let people know about special author visitations to attract customers. Think of beauty salons that can use the apps for promotion by letting fashionistas everywhere to know about the latest fashion trends in the market. Even the retail shops can expand their overall business by sending out promotional discounts and a quick guide about their latest inventory.

Once you reflect upon these points, start brainstorming ways in which you can use a mobile app for your own business. In this segment, I will show you the benefits of mobile apps and how they can be used in your day-to-day activities in terms of sales and lead generation. You should care because technology is evolving fast, time and development cycles have compressed significantly, and you don't want to be left behind.

Barely anyone can keep up with the sweeping changes that are occurring every day in this flourishing industry. It's a daunting challenge, but nevertheless a very exciting and thrilling one to watch; where it's taking us no-one can tell. The future is now and it's mobile! You could potentially lose money if you're not following the trends and anticipating markets. In this segment we are going to expose them. Last, but not least, you should take action once you are convinced that A) a mobile app can help you with sales, B) it can expand your reach, C) it will help connect with clients and D) you will have a better understanding of who your target audience is. So let's dive into it.

The first things you will notice on a mobile application are the background images and the navigation menu. The design and look of your app is meant to grab users' attention and convey the theme of what your application is about. You want to engage them on multiple fronts and good designs are meant to stand out and sell. Businesses should be aware of the fact that for an app to be successful, the app must ensure integration of certain key concepts to garner the attention of the public. In short, widespread marketing campaigns could easily fail if apps fail to be user-friendly. By adhering to the following four influential characteristics of a user-friendly app, businesses can rest assured that they are on the right path to a successful penetration of the mobile market.

1) Think On The Go — Statistics claim that 90 percent of the time, users will be in motion and on the go while utilizing your app. Thus, keep it simple. Forgo placing redundant and unnecessary information in your app; people can visit your website for detailed information. Certify that your app is directive and to the point so that people can embrace it for its simplicity.

2)   In-app User Interface (UI) — The UI of an app basically refers to the ease with which the programming of an app interacts with the end-user. For example, the display screen, placement buttons, screen orientation and even color scheme all play a role in app-user interaction. A poorly designed UI can affect the overall value and effectiveness of your app. Thus, it should be your primary focus to guarantee a well-designed and innovative UI.

3)   Smaller Screen Real Estate — Unlike your laptops and desktops, mobile devices have limits in terms of the availability of network bandwidth and screen space. When designing your app, these constraints should be catered for in order to improve the overall user experience of your app.

4)   User Experience (UX) — The UX is about the longevity of the app. It drives sales, downloads and great reviews in the app stores. It's mainly responsible for the engagement the app is capable of garnering from its users. App developers need to know what the triggers for their target market are, and what appeals to their highest lifetime value users and give it to them.

These are just a few things to consider when designing a mobile app, but there are plenty more to think about once you get going. Secondly, you want to raise customer interest with your app by demonstrating features, benefits, and advantages of whatever you are selling. There are many ways to do it depending on what it is that you are selling and who your target audience is. If you already have a happy and loyal customer base, you want to leverage that trust to land even more clients inside your business with your app. Third, there's a correlation that exists between customer retention and user's experience when it comes to apps and mobile marketing. You want to convince customers that your business is more than just desirable and that you can really satisfy their needs. I'm suggesting building a lasting bond on both ends, one that transcends the casual business-customer relationship. You want to do this A) because that's a feature and B) because it's a known fact that people like to buy from people they like and trust. So, why not take advantage of this unique opportunity to build your trust and likability? You will stand out when none of your competitors are doing this.

Happy customers are repeat buyers; these are the same people who will entice others to try out "their" new amazing app out of the thrill and excitement of knowing they stumbled upon a rare gem no-one else has. Finally, once they become happy customers, you can lead your customers towards taking a specific and measurable action at a 90% success rate. Your mobile application is a multimedia cutting edge versatile sales weapon that's precisely capable of that. It combines text, imagery, sound and video as ways of engaging clients on multiple levels. You have the power to trigger instant sales within seconds by sending out tweets and SMS text ads that will land in customers' pockets or handbags, bypassing traditional, costly third-party services such as newspapers, magazines, radio or TV.

Exact Target reports that 16% of Smartphone users report that they have made a purchase as a result of a marketing message they received on their phone. Fifty-five percent purchased as a result of an email they received on their mobile device. You can also grow your audience by leaps and bounds in ways unheard of exponentially with social media. This is what this technology is capable of! It has slashed the physical boundaries of marketing to the ground and buried them to oblivion, because there are none in the virtual world. However, with new territories come new responsibilities, and you should be mindful on how you wish to use it. A bad tweet or the wrong picture could send the wrong message, easily tarnishing your image and reputation, and this could potentially cost you sales and customers. So in this respect, a word of caution: Be wise.

In the next segment I will walk you through the main features you can find inside a mobile app for business. Upwards of 30 functions and more can be coded inside your mobile application based on your unique specifications and personal preferences. You can import entire websites inside your app, create stores and catalogs, create image galleries, upload videos, create PDF files people can download and share, and even add a car finder feature, for instance, which people can use to spot their car in a huge parking lot. If you can think of a feature that can help grow your business exponentially, demand it and we shall build it.

Home Page Tab

The home page tab is basically a tab with your business contact information with a tap-to-call button, directions, and "tell-a-friend" functionalities. All your basic information is accessible from this one page. If you have more than just one location, you can expand this feature to list them. You can add as many locations as you want with contact information such as telephone number, address, website, map location and email address. This tab can be a directory to multiple sites.

Regarding designs and layouts, you can customize and brand your mobile app to your specific needs with impressive logos and slogans. Attention grabbing graphics and catchy slogans are far more engaging than graphics that are not, as they are entertaining.

Anything that gets people's attention, i.e. getting people using, sharing and reviewing your app is worthwhile exploiting to the fullest. Apps with a ton of feedback and social engagement move up in the search results much quicker inside the app stores. The app stores pick those social signals real fast (they love interaction), and all of a sudden your app is no longer on page 50, but has jumped up to page 1, or somewhere near that.

Contact Tab with Multiple Sites

Around Us Tab

The Around Us tab is a map location tab whose main functionality is to highlight 3 major locations in your area, marked in colors you want to appear on the map. It has no relevant function other than pinpointing other businesses and locations of interest for customers on the map in your area.

This map application helps situate your customer with directions by highlighting specific locations in your area, pertaining either to your business or their interest. If you have a big audience to your name, you can use this tab for ad placements and sell those spots to the highest bidders in your area.

Menu Tab

This application is the window to your products and services. It allows you to display menus à la carte for restaurants and create categories and submenus inside your app. You can create breakfast, lunch, and dinner menus, etc., and have submenus such as soup, salad, meat, pastas, wines, etc. This tab can be used to list items other than food as well. This tab allows your customers to access your entire menu with pictures and description without having to call you up, or searching the Internet to get this information. This allows them to know what's on the menu before leaving home. You can update this tab any time you want with new offers.

Mobile Food Ordering Tab

Product Display & Description

Add to Cart / Place Order

If you are a pizza or restaurant owner with a food delivery service, this tab comes in pretty handy. You can create entire order pages customers can utilize to order their favorite food and dishes without leaving home or calling in. You can import your entire menu listings inside this tab with menus, categories, subcategories, pictures, and descriptions. It utilizes an integrated shopping cart which accepts PayPal payments, credit card, or you can cash in on delivery, if you choose so.

This tab can be used to create order pages for all sorts of products and services besides food and beverage, such as clothing, fashion, furniture, antiques, second hand articles, memorabilia, etc. You can import entire product lines and have them displayed in categories, subcategories, and submenus with pictures and descriptions. This is a great plus for businesses because the buying/selling capability becomes an integral part of your app, which simplifies many processes for you and your customers. Your customers' buying experience is greatly enhanced, giving them the sense of having more power and freedom with their pocket Smartphones.

Mailing List Tab

The email list tab is designed to create a database of your clients and is essential for many reasons. First, it helps you with sales since you can email new offers to your entire list, or remind them to take action with discounts, coupons and special offers, when needed. Second, it gives you the ability to better connect with clients in the sense that you can keep them updated with relevant information pertaining to your business.

Customers have a better understanding of whom you are, how your business works and what to expect. Third, you can drill a little bit deeper in your understanding of who your target audience is. You can create forms with multiple fields, drop-down menus, check boxes, message fields, etc., allowing you to run customer satisfaction surveys and do instant market research. With this extra knowledge, you can expand your market reach and understand how you can increase your bottom line and create new products.

The benefit of this application is that it allows you to collect key vital information customers never told you before and to segment your list into multiple categories for a better understanding of your market. This way, you can make better offers; create new products, craft better messages and charge more if this is what your data is suggesting to you. It's essential for successful product launches.

Let's say, for example, you released a new pizza creation and you want some feedback from your launch. You want to know if they liked the extra garlic, the onions, the paprika, the salmon, the pepperoni, even the name and layout you came up with, or if they have better ideas and suggestions. You can email your list, or send a SMS text asking them to take a survey and hit the submit button. When they reply, you will instantly know if your last ploy was a hit or not. You will be able to improve your product based on recommendations and charge more if this is what your information is telling you.

For product launches, you can drill down much deeper in your quest for knowledge, and expanding on this, you can create an entire image gallery of your latest T-shirts and fashion designs, your latest ring designs, tattoo designs if you have a clothing shop, you're a jeweler, run a tattoo shop, etc. and ask them to tell you which designs they prefer and why.

Out of 1,000 people surveyed, 298 may say they like design A with the Statue of Liberty in the case of the clothing shop, because of the top notch graphic designs and colorful slogan, 549 could say they prefer design B with George Washington, Thomas Jefferson and JFK because these are modern liberty iconic figures, with only 153 preferring the Snoopy design. Instantly you would know that design B is a winner for your next product launch, and so you could send to your list a 30% off limited special promotion coupon for 5 days, or for the first 150 T-shirts sold to kickstart sales. No other marketing channel be it TV, radio, or print, is capable of collecting this kind of information first-hand, this fast, and with such lethal precision. This feature will teach you new skills and help you develop new strategies through this form of intelligence collection.

If you have a bigger brand like Starbucks, you can bypass this process entirely and create an entire page inside your app designed specifically to this end, where customers will breed thoughts and ideas on ways to improve your products and services for you. Ask and let the market speak! Starbucks runs, for example, a networking site called MyStarbucksIdea.com, where they go to customers basically for new product ideas. They don't have to look to the stars when designing their next product; they use their database of a million users instead. Whether you have millions of fans like Starbucks or not, this tab will provide you with the necessary information to run your operation successfully, be it large or small.

Scan the QR code below to see how customer satisfaction surveys work inside a mobile app.

Video: http://youtu.be/A4_IViM2bOM

Messages Tab

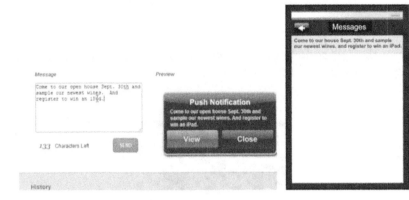

The Message tab functionality, better known as "push-notification," is like email list building on steroids. This feature gives you the capability to send messages to your audience straight to their cell phones. If you want to utilize the marketing potential of your app, this is the main feature you will want to use daily to send 140 character messages to broadcast whatever offers you want to send to your customers.

This feature is the pendant to SMS text messaging you will use regularly to drive foot traffic inside your business. It costs nothing to send push-notifications whereas SMS text messaging is a third party service not related to apps. Restaurants will love this application because it allows them to fill the void caused by slow days, by sending out special offers, coupons, and other freebies to lure clients. Businesses with perishable and non-perishable goods will love this feature too because it allows them to liquidate unsold inventory and quickly recoup their initial investment. The same goes for businesses relying heavily on volume and traffic to stay afloat over the month.

Social Media

Your mobile app has built-in social media capabilities to connect with your target audience on 4 of the most trafficked websites on the Internet: Facebook, YouTube, Twitter, and LinkedIn. More social networking sites can be added and this feature will help you in many ways.

First, you will bond with customers on 2 of the most viral websites on the Internet, namely Facebook and Twitter. These networks are giant hives of interconnected people on the Internet, meaning whatever happens in your area can spread overnight nationwide! Second, any engagement you receive from your app will send signals to the app stores showing how often your app was downloaded, opened, for how long, etc. This will boost your rankings and downloads tremendously because the app stores will notice the value and usefulness of your app and push you up. The app stores rely on many factors to gauge the value of an app, and social engagements top the list! Any tweet or post shared on Facebook will show up in people's feeds, resulting in more traffic, increased exposure and boosting your rankings inside the app stores.

Also, the ability people have of accessing your social profiles from their cell phones is very unique. They need not wait to get home to interact with you; they can do it from their car, at the mall, during an appointment, between the breaks, or when eating. People love the magic of interaction especially when they can inject their thoughts and impact others in a meaningful way. If you want to avoid all the noise on Facebook and Twitter and keep the interaction in-house, it can be done. You can set up a fan wall inside your application that's only privy to you and your customers. The app stores will still pick the social engagement coming from your app but you will not get traffic and referrals coming from Facebook or Twitter.

Other tools that engage customers in a meaningful way and that will get social signals for you are the email photo tab and the voice recorder tab. The email photo tab allows you to share unique moments with friends and family. Say you're a client and you're enjoying your favorite meal; you can take pictures and post them on the fan wall for others to see. If you're the business owner, you can reward the best picture with a free lunch, or a bottle of Dom Pérignon at the end of the week.

You're having fun in your favorite nightclub; you can share those unforgettable moments for friends to see. Your local bar is organizing a sport event with music bands and karaoke music? Same deal, take a picture and share all that excitement for the whole world to see. Maybe you were involved in a car accident where you were clearly not at fault, take a picture and send it to your DUI lawyer. This may be the piece of evidence that will help you win your court case. When these pictures are associated with your business, this is the kind of unsolicited attention sponsored by your own customers that you get.

The voice recorder is an interactive functionality that allows customers to record short messages they can send you over email from their cell phones. You can ask customers for testimonials you can share on your blog, which is the social proof to the kinds of products and services that you sell. If you are a bartender, you can stage karaoke song contests with this tab and let people win prizes in a draw of the month, for example. If you're a lawyer, this can be very useful to get oral witness accounts used as piece of evidence from eye witnesses involved in a crime, car accident, or whatever the case is. Both functionalities allow you to better connect with clients, let you have a deeper understanding of who your target audience is, and with social media you can expand your reach, thus allowing you to make even more sales.

110

Voice Recorder Tab

Yelp Tab

With this tab, you have access to the most trusted review site on the Web — Yelp! You can pull any information you want pertaining to your business just like you would see it on your desktop PC. You can navigate the entire website without having to leave your application. Your customers can see how your business is rated, how to contact you, and can use it to post reviews for others to see.

This application puts your business in the limelight of third party reviews, adding transparency to your business. Customers have the ability to rate your business from this application. We recommend, however, utilizing this tab in conjunction with a comment capture system and a citation management system when collecting reviews from clients. Your business gets more referrals and has better reviews and ratings on other prominent websites such as Yellow Pages, InsiderPages, etc., just let us know and we'll feature those websites for you instead.

We've covered a few features in this chapter. There are more than these 8 functionalities we can code for you. If you want to learn more, you can reach out to our support desk for a 1-on-1 consultation — the information is provided to you at the end of the book.

PART THREE: DOWNLOADS, SALES & TRAFFIC

In this section, we show you how to get downloads. We show the significance of an optimized app inside the app stores and why dominating the local searches, to drive sales and traffic, is essential.

How to Get Downloads

Depending on your budget, there are 2 ways of running your app marketing campaign. The cost-effective solution utilizes flyers, local ads, banners, merchandizing, mobile website, local search optimization, and social media whereas businesses with deeper pockets may consider hiring app agencies and running ads on TV and billboards. If your app campaign is about branding, loyalty, reputation, etc., you are talking about long term strategy and you need to plan for the long haul. On the other hand, if your campaign is about sales, you can go either way, depending on your budget situation.

Espresso Macchiato

What's the Plan?

Do you know how many your target audience is in numbers and how to reach them? It's critical to have a plan before hitting the ground running to avoid a waste of your time, resources, and energy. There are 3 factors that speak for a successful app in the app stores: A) a quality app, B) your app caters to a rabid market, and C) a good marketing plan. If your app is not in one of these categories and wasn't lucky to make it to the top, it simply doesn't exist. People find your app inside the app stores with keywords; because your app was the pick of the month, or because they just stumbled upon it.

There's literally a myriad of apps, thousands upon thousands waiting to be discovered inside the app stores with thousands more being added everyday. These apps are developed by corporations, tech giants with financial capabilities and manpower to back them, including small businesses and private individuals. You'd think each app was downloaded once in its lifespan and has the exposure it truly deserves; this is the popular common belief. Actually, you'd be quite shocked how many apps go unnoticed, majority of them! App developers who care to treat their apps like a business are very successful with each new launch. These are the people who are making a fortune on Smartphones, they are savvy entrepreneurs with a clear vision and a laser focus and who have a fundamental understanding of the input and output mechanism that governs any business. They make the little club of the 2%. Frankly, there's no reason why this figure should be a bit higher. If you're looking to the stars for answers and wonder why your app never finds a user, then you're definitely on the other side of the fence with the rest 98%, and procrastinating won't help either.

The reason why app developers fail 98% of the time is because they lack the marketing (i.e. proper planning and funding) needed to succeed with their app in the app stores. They have a vague idea and a narrow view about the app stores and how they truly work. They sincerely believe that once they make it inside, it's game over, when in all certainty they should be actually pushing hard their apps. They assume that a magic lightning bolt will strike their app to riches, when nothing happens randomly in the app stores. Without any mistake, the law of the jungle applies to the app stores too; this is the new Wild West!

The hardest part in developing an app is not the coding but the marketing. They need to figure out ways to make their app stand out and make it sell, when organically, the discovery process has failed them. A strong analogy you can draw from the real world is that of a newborn baby, you have to spank upside down to get it breathing. You need to feed it until it can eat and walk by itself as well. Can you imagine for one second what would happen if you failed to take these basic steps? Very gruesome thoughts indeed, yet this is the part that's often neglected. This is why only 2% of the apps make it to the top and enjoy the kind of ROI the rest 98% can only dream of.

With well over 850,000 apps and counting developed since 2007, there's literally a gold rush in the app stores and businesses need good marketing skills to stand out from the competition, or risk falling flat on their faces, with more apps being developed every day, one being better than the original. If you spend $2,000 or $50,000 developing an app, your marketing budget should be at least double the developing costs and failure to allocate those funds is a recipe for total disaster and why most of them fail.

Fig. 2.1 Gold Rush in The 1850s

Quality Apps
Apple has stringent guidelines your app needs to fulfill to be downloaded by your target audience. Apple values quality apps that offer a great user experience, great functionality, and top notch graphic designs. When you fail to meet those criteria, this can result in the rejection of your application inside the app store. Not many app developers and businesses are aware of this, which explains why a significant number of applications inside the Apple store are rejected.

According to Tim Cook, CEO of Apple, out of the 26,000 applications submitted for review each week, 30 percent are

117

rejected for failure to meet developer guidelines. That's a huge number, and once rejected it's an uphill battle you have to win to convince the gatekeepers that your app is worthy of being hosted just as the other apps they allow in are. In the worst case scenario, you can give up and blame bad luck for the misfortune and in the best case scenario, you could scrap your app, learn from your mistakes, go back to the drawing boards and resubmit it again with a new name, a new description and a new face. The top 9 reasons mobile apps get rejected from the Apple App Store are: the use of the word "beta" or otherwise indicating that your app is unfinished, long load time, linking to outside payment schemes, failure to mention other supported platforms, localization glitches, improper use of storage and file systems, crashes from users denying permissions to other services, improper use of icons and buttons and misuse of trademarks and logos.

Knowing this information will spare you headaches, frustrations and wasted time that leave you often disillusioned and desperate. Apps that utilize native features have a better chance of approval than apps that don't use any. The look and feel of your app can be a reason for rejection as well. When the background images are poorly designed or look cheap, this sends the wrong signal and Apple will reject them outright. Similarly, apps that have a tendency to crash will be turned off immediately and this is why you should seek the guidance of specialists in the field before tempting the devil and risking a flat out rejection. Google, in comparison, is too permissive with applications, which is why their submission rate is much higher than Apple and people can get away basically with any sin with Google, but not with Apple.

App Submission
When you submit your app inside the app stores, you need to provide the following information before your app is approved: your app name, app description, the app category and keyword list, your app icon, etc. and this is where things get tricky!

Submitting this information alone constitutes no guarantee that your app will be discovered or will sell. Just like for the search engines, there's a lot of work that goes into optimizing your app to get clicks and downloads. That's why app stores should be viewed as mini search engines because that's what they really are. Below is a list of key factors you need to tweak and optimize to increase your visibility and downloads:

1. Descriptive name
2. High definition eye catching icon
3. High converting app store content
4. Clean user friendly app website

The name of your app, for instance, has to be catchy, memorable, preferably short, and says what the app does. Preferably, you want to use a keyword rich name that describes your business, highlights the benefits of the app, that's fun or that's very easy to remember. Next, you need to have a kick-ass high definition icon that drives clicks. An eye catching, well-crafted icon that says unmistakably and unequivocally what your app is about will drive traffic with a lot less words better than one that doesn't and instead leaves the user clueless and guessing. A well-crafted description will do the selling for you. The description should list the benefits and features of your app and give compelling reasons why the user should pick your app over the competition. Part of your job is to underline the unique selling proposition of the app and what sets your app apart from the competition. For example, if a user sees your app and asks, "what's in it for **_me_**?" you should give them reasons to download your app and share it with others in your unique selling proposition. If you can address their pain, for example, and demonstrate what the app can do for them, you fill a need that will help you sell more apps. People also like compelling stories behind a product and service; they like to relate to events, people, and experiences and if you can connect with them on a deeper level, you increase the likelihood of getting downloads dramatically. Is there any story or personal experience that triggered your app into existence? If so, state it!

The example of two kids selling lemonade on a street corner, in the subway, etc., next to a vending machine is one I can't stop thinking of to make my case. People like buying from vending machines to quench their thirst because of the broad choice of beverages they have. However, it's the spirit of entrepreneurship, the idea of independence, of starting a business with something so little like lemonades that will compel them

119

to stop and reward those kids for their efforts because people can relate to the hard work, patience, commitment, and struggle of these two kids, whereas the sophisticated soulless vending machine next to them has none.

For instance, if you go back to page xiii of this book you learn about the genesis of this book and how it came to existence, from there you will discover the story of a guy and his struggle to connect with his target audience. You will learn the challenges he faced while attempting to demonstrate the worth and usefulness of a mobile app for local businesses to generate leads over the phone, which by all intent and purpose was far from easy and very challenging in some situations. You will also learn how he was resolute in resolving this issue. This is a piece of information I thought was worthwhile mentioning right from the outset. It adds perspective and helps the reader understand the information he is about to receive bit by bit. If people are appreciative of this book, they will give thanks to this little introduction that this book offers, because it was a response to a dire situation. This shows that every little piece of information no matter how little or insignificant you think it is in your product description really counts.

Here are just a few questions you can ask yourself to know what a compelling and well-crafted unique selling proposition should look like. A thorough examination of these items will help you find your own USP:

1. What are the benefits and features of the app?
2. Who is your competition?
3. What makes your app unique?
4. What's your personal story?

An example of a USP is the legendary *"30 minutes delivery or it's free"* by pizza giant, Domino's. If this is not a compelling argument to buy pizzas, I don't know what is! Delivered express in less than 30 minutes or yours free to keep — very practical when you're hungry and in a hurry. How many pizzas did they sell? According to research,[29] they grossed $1 billion dollars with this catchy promise alone.

---

[29] http://www.interactivemarketinginc.com/unique-selling-proposition.html

There are more examples on site to copy from. If you can see how it works, I'm sure you can come up with some very creative ideas to set your business apart from the competition and set your app on fire. Mapping out your competition in your local area and knowing their strengths and weaknesses will give you a competitive edge; you need to get those click through rates. Below, you can see an example of an app using a nice icon, a good name, and that leverages reviews to get clicks:

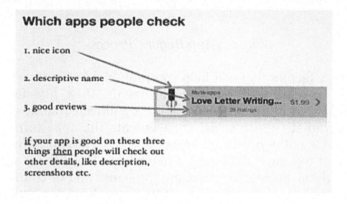

Fig. 2.2 Good Name, Good Icon and Top Reviews

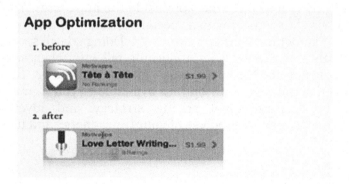

Fig. 2.3 App Optimization – Before and After

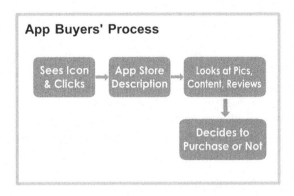

Fig. 2.4 App Buyers' Process

Other factors that will help you rank highly are search key-words, reviews and social engagements. Just like for any product sold online, reviews play a significant role in getting clicks, but it's those social engagements the app stores pick fast, such as the open rate, usage duration, in-app purchases, etc., that top the list! There are many ways to get those signals fast without necessarily breaking the bank, and of course, the more positive reviews you have, the better. Knowing these factors will position your app higher in the app stores and expand your reach. This is what you need to know, in a nutshell, about submitting and selling your app inside the app stores. You are well advised to consult with a specialist before submitting your app and launching your app campaign. Doing so will spare you the costly mistakes 98% of applicants fall into when submitting their app for the first time inside the app stores. Besides that, you should know all options available to you to make an informed decision about pricing, strategy, and advertising platforms, to make a good use of your time, energy and money.

Working with Professionals

In this chapter, we shall discuss what to look for when marketing your app inside the app stores and the qualities an app marketer or app consultant should have to assist you. Because of the explosion of the market, first off, I must say that app marketers and app consultants are rare breeds, whom are in big demand. Very few people have ventured into this space to cope with the rapid growth this has caused. You will find some companies providing help and support to app developers; they are few and far between and you will have to search deep to find the ones you feel comfortable working with.

Who Counts as a Professional and Who Doesn't?

The first thing to look for is whether or not this consultant has knowledge about apps, the app stores and the Internet. If he doesn't, don't bother pursuing talks because neither a sales representative with a college degree is up to the task, nor will an Internet marketer with no inside knowledge will help you because, well, you need both and some experience in the field.

If he has designed and uploaded apps before, you should definitely get in touch with him. His skill set should encompass SEO, PPC, social media, and Internet marketing in a broad sense. He should have good copywriter skills, have a good eye for graphic designs, and be fluent in 1 or more foreign languages preferably if your app campaign has an international reach. If he uses offline methods such as TV, print, billboards, etc., besides the Internet to push your app, this is also a great plus. Second, he needs to understand the Apple and Android stores, and understand how app store optimization (ASO) works. These are the basic requirements to look for before establishing some work relationship and entrusting him with your app marketing campaign.

How to Find Them?

Start your search with Google and don't look inside the Yellow Pages for answers because you won't find them there. When searching, location shouldn't be your main focus because A) supply is low and B) as far as the rankings and downloads go, it is not relevant. The app stores are opened to the public worldwide and what counts are the downloads you'll get rather than the location of whomever you're working with. This is what your primary focus should center on.

Outsourcing sites are great venues to prospect as well; however, finding a good match is a real challenge for the simple reason that this trade is brand new. In your project description, you should outline what the app is about, say who your target audience is, the date of release, number of app downloads you're targeting, etc. If you don't have an app developed yet, you may consider posting this project to find programmers willing to design a mobile app for your business.

Finding good programmers is yet another hurdle to overcome and you will need good judgment to assess who's fit for the job when auditing. Prices for developing apps vary, they can be as low as $500 and upward; there's no limit. You can spend somewhere between $5,000 and $100,000 or more, depending on what your needs are. One thing to look for when the app is developed is to test it through a third party for its functionality to see if it really works and to make sure it doesn't crash. This is critical. If it doesn't, you need to tweak it and improve it until it works flawlessly. Once it has passed this hurdle, the next is getting it approved inside the app stores. This is where you need to know what makes an app valuable in the eyes of Apple. In fact, you should look for this information prior to developing it in order to spare yourself from unpleasant surprises and unexpected situations. Once your app has passed this hurdle yet again, this is where you will need services of app consultants to tweak it and optimize it in and outside the app stores.

What to Expect from Consultations with App Consultants?

In this short segment, I will give you a general walkthrough of what to expect from consultations with an expert so that you can be prepared and not become overwhelmed by the process. Ideally, before meeting with an app consultant, you should set your goals first. Do you want more sales, better customer retention, bigger market shares, build a list, do market research,

124

get traffic, branding yourself, etc.? Second, you need to know how many downloads you want in terms of sales and lead generation, and know who your competition is so the app consultant has some elements to work with. If you can research this information prior to the meeting, this will ease up a lot of things. With this information, your app consultant will dig deeper and assess your needs.

Based on your location, your industry, your niche, the size of your market, your target audience, client surf habits, competition, website, your budget, etc., he will come with best recommendations. He will draft a marketing proposal that fits your criteria and will help you with downloads. Next, if you agree to the plan and terms of the contract, he will invoice the total expense based on the duration of the campaign and amount of work involved. Such work includes keyword research and keyword analysis, content creation, app landing page, SEO, PPC, and social media, video marketing, reputation marketing, icon designs, app description, app screenshots, etc., not to mention the design and development of the app, just in case you don't have one.

Prices for standard business apps vary between $1,500 and $5,000, depending on the level of specifications and time needed to develop them. If you're looking to develop unique specifications than the ones outlined in this book, it can be done. Get in touch with us so we can hammer out the details of your unique mobile application.

As a rule of thumb, you should set aside a bare minimum of 2 to 3 times more funds for marketing than what your app costs you to develop. This may seem a lot; however, bear in mind that this is the surest way to get it downloaded and long term, your advertising costs will drop significantly. You will recoup your initial investment based on the savings you will make on traditional outbound marketing because of the repeat sales you'll be able to generate on the backend from your campaigns, the viral reach of your app, market research and the kind of feedback you'll get first-hand from clients, and the ability you will have to retain customers long term.

If you compare the cost and return of traditional marketing vs. that of mobile marketing, it's like comparing night and day or a 100-year-old tractor to a V10 new Lamborghini Gallardo with all the bells and whistles; there is no comparison.

With an app, you're in touch with your customers 24/7. This is not possible with other types of advertising channels. You can't leave your TV set or radio on for 24 hours just to make sure you won't miss an ad. This would be a hazard not only to your health, but you would feel the impact in your pockets too. However, with an app, you will never miss out on special offers that were sent out to you at any given time. If you don't have a budget for marketing, this option may not be for you. If you're spending a bare minimum of $500 a month to land new clients, you should consider this option and compare it with other forms of advertisement you're currently using to see which one benefits you more in terms of sales and lead generation. What's more effective is that it's a one-time install you can leverage ad infinitum with cheap push-notifications and SMS text messaging, coupon codes, special offers and super discounts. Costly print and TV ads are less effective in comparison because you can't tweak and track them, as they are intrusive.

Let's say, for example, you're a restaurant owner and your app was downloaded 15,000 times from your initial launch. Of that, 2,000 were old customers, 6,000 were new customers and the rest, 7,000, were app enthusiasts, prospects, and potential leads who got wind of the launch. You can segment this list into 3 main categories and craft messages targeting them.

To your old customers, you will thank them and stage some event to show them how your app works. To your new customers, you will welcome them on board with special offers and super discounts just to get them excited, and to your third group, you will seek ways to bring them into the fold long term, or use them to get more referrals. But right off the bat, you have a list of 8,000 people to work with; you can send offers any time of the day and get new leads virally with your app.

What is a client worth for you and how many sales can you make off of them? The 6,000 new customers you were able to land in this example from the initial launch have paid off for the app costs in one strike. If your customers spend $30 on average for a meal, that's an extra $180,000 at the least you can book per month. Assuming you landed just a fraction of it, like 1,000 new customers, that's a $30,000 sales increase per month and you can envisage all sorts of possibilities you can do with your app.

Marketing Rollout

It takes roughly 2 weeks to work out the details of a marketing plan with a market, budget, and competition analysis, approximately 4 weeks to design a business app, with app description, screenshots and icon, etc., 1-2 weeks to get approved inside the app stores, and 2 to 6 months to roll out the marketing plan. There's a lot of consulting that goes on, back and forth, to make the necessary tweaks and changes, and Apple charges you a yearly fee of $99 and Google $25 for listing your app inside their store. Once your app has received the downloads you wanted, the fulfillment part with your app consultant is done and you can carry onward with your marketing or hire a virtual assistant to manage sales, your SMS and social media campaigns. A good app consultant will recommend you good virtual assistants if you have none to work with, or he may take on the job if you want to hire him. You can reach out to us; this is a service we offer.

Scan this QR code[30] to take part in the final quiz:

The 4 Rs

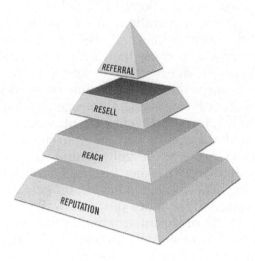

Fig. 2.5 "Reputation, Reach, Resell & Referral"

There are 4 major pillars any business needs to work on every day to grow their business. These are Reputation, market Reach, Resells and Referrals. Each pillar is equally important to the success of a business and it's the synergetic and compounded effect of these separate units that will spearhead your marketing efforts and reward you with increased sales and a positive ROI. Leave one unit out of the equation and your efforts will come crumbling down.

Since the advent of social media and citation sites, we live in a reputation economy, where every facet of a business is scrutinized for good or bad, leaving no room for speculation and the benefit of a doubt. Your reputation, market reach, resell and referrals are key performance indicators to look after when it comes to selling products and services with a mobile app. Do you know A) if your reputation is working for you or against you? B) How many fresh leads do you land on a monthly basis? C) Do you have additional cross-sell offers besides your core product? And D) are clients actively sending you referrals?

Your reputation online is worth its weight in gold, it's your personal online brand and brands are what differentiate products and businesses from one another. Everyone knows what the Adidas, Nike, Disney, Sony, Coca-Cola and Mercedes-Benz brands are. These corporations need no introduction; they have established reputations and need no extra reinforcement to draw huge crowds because their name recognition is a moneymaker no matter where you go in the world. A regular mom and pop shop down the street certainly do need introduction because it doesn't have this name recognition like these large companies. Therefore, your skills, talent, wisdom, experience, leadership and reputation become your hard currency and hard assets you can trade for money online. It is invaluable.

Your reputation drives sales; this is the foundation to your success online. The more reputable you get, the more your currency grows, and the more your sales will soar. Conversely, when there's little or no information available to sway opinions, people will dismiss you automatically because you are an unknown entity and they don't like messing with things they hardly know anything about. Here's a little exercise I want you to do: type the following keywords into Google: "plumbers in Yonkers NY," "plumbers in Saratoga Springs NY," "plumbers in London Ontario" to illustrate my case."

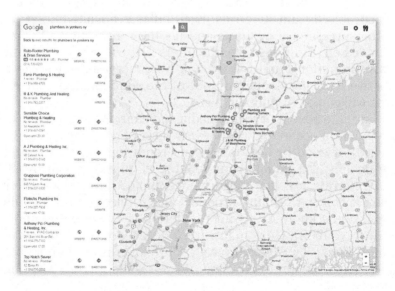

Plumbers in Yonkers, New York

The results show that 2 of 36 plumbers in Yonkers, New York, 3 of 13 in Saratoga Springs, and 4 of 42 in London, Ontario have reviews. In this example you can see why the majority of these businesses are losing money online: there's no information at all. This total lack of information and transparency is the reason why most visitors stay away from these businesses. It clutters potential clients with riddles and thick clouds of opacity, which tells you that they don't know what they're doing, or are simply careless. They don't know which way the wind is blowing. This is reckless behavior because these businesses are losing a lot of money online — wittingly or unwittingly.

Judging by their profiles, you can sense that they are not Internet savvy. Otherwise, they would not leave the door wide open for speculation. Imagine walking down the block passing these businesses and 90% of them saying "open," yet looking inside they are empty, dusty and in shambles. Would you walk inside? Probably not. Yet, this is the impression they leave online. It's not a friendly warm one! Often, I hesitate contacting these businesses; it's become second nature and a knee-jerk reaction. Why bother knocking on their door when the competition is giving me more reasons to spend money online with them is what I ask myself each time.

"We Are Open"

131

I know their plight, yet it's a tough call to pick up the phone with so little feedback. First off, you wonder why they have no reviews and if they can be trusted. The lesson you can draw from this little example is this: If you don't assert control over your reputation online, others will by default. You will lose money and your reputation to others who will gladly assert it for you. This is how the game is played.

This is why a reputable company always attracts good clients willing to pay good money for quality goods and services, whereas a bad reputation online or lack thereof is simply a business killer. Easy access to information on the Internet gives anyone around the world the power to decide where they want to spend their money, and one of the key indicators people seek first besides price and product description, is your reputation.

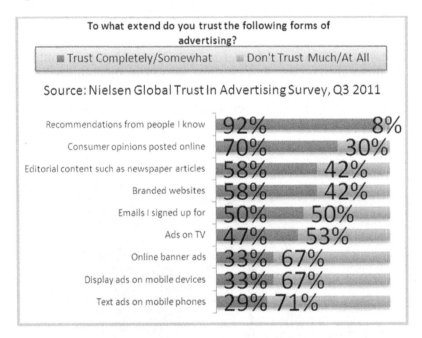

Fig. 2.6 "70% trust customer opinions posted online" –
Nielsen Global Trust, 2011

Studies show that 70% of people surveyed trust a business based on other people's recommendations online, and this information shows where your focus should be when building your business online. You can outrank your competition all day every day in the search engines and create a good online presence, yet have a bad or poor reputation, which means no one will do business with you because money goes where the good stuff is. Once you've built a reputable foundation for your business, you can work on your rankings to increase traffic. Your market reach is all about lead generation. What is your current lead generation strategy, how successful are you and which feature is likely to drive sales inside your app? Your app has the capability to collect reviews from your customers with a comment capture page built in. Part of your activities should consist of collecting reviews daily; measure their impact relative to your lead generation strategy and to spy on your competition. These are key questions you can ask yourself and develop strategies:

1. How is their lead generation different from mine?
2. How can I use it in my business?
3. What are their weaknesses, can I exploit them?
4. What are the surf habits of their customers and how can I target them online and offline?
5. Can I use my app to spy on the competition?
6. Can I use my app to steal customers away from the competition?

The third R is about resells, once you have a sales funnel in place to land clients. You need to maximize the lifetime value of your customer rather than just land one client after the other. There are 3 ways to increase profits for any business and these are getting more clients, increase profits per sale and increase the frequency of sale. This is done with up-sells and cross-sells, by creating new streams of income with new products and services, monthly programs and add-on services. You can make repeat sales with a good CRM system in place and that's precisely why a mobile app is such a key vital tool in the life cycle of your business.

The 4th and last R is about referrals. When you're very good at what you do, the logical step is to ask for referrals. Most clients won't refer you other people however, even when they're 100% happy with your service. So you need to encourage them because referrals add more business and they help you save money on marketing and advertisement. According to a case study noted in the Harvard Business Review, referred customers are, on average, about 18% more likely than others to stay with a company and they generate 16% more in profits. These are compelling arguments your business can greatly benefit from. What type of incentives are you currently using to get referrals and how you go about it with an app?

A mobile app will help you leverage these 4 pillars in a very decisive way. In the following table, you can see how it all works perfectly together and how you can leverage each one of these pillars to maximize sales and increase your ROI exponentially. Please get in touch with us if you need implementing a winning strategy inside your mobile app.

Reputation	Reach	Resell	Referral
Comment Capture Page	Flyers & Banners	Email Marketing	Email Marketing
Citation Management System	Local Ads	Push-Notifications	Push-Notifications
	Local SEO	SMS Marketing	SMS Marketing
	ASO	Social Media	Social Media
	App Marketing		

Leveraging the 4 Rs with a Mobile App

Managing Your Reputation with Your Mobile App

You can create a comment capture page inside your app and encourage customers to give you testimonials when they visit you. This allows you to exert control on what's being said about your business online and you can correct the wrongs when they arise, and root out those negative comments from the positive before they show up elsewhere online. You can show customers how to download your app with a QR code scan inside your business and ask them for a feedback before walking out of your shop, or you can give them forms where they can rate your business, just in case they can't scan the QR code.

With a comment capture system and citation management system built in, you can address grievances for damage control and for a better service monitoring. This is how you can make good use of reputation management. Obviously, there's more to reputation management and reputation marketing than I can squeeze inside this little chapter, but basically, this is what a business app can help you achieve and how you can monitor and leverage your reputation online and build a rock solid foundation for your business.

Mobile App Comment Capture Page

A mobile app will expand your reach with app downloads in the app stores, through social media, by leveraging Google Maps traffic, and by displaying your app QR codes anywhere around you. This is how you can have a bigger market penetration on mobile devices. With sufficient downloads you can sell, up-sell, and cross-sell your customers all day every day and generate new streams of income utilizing push-notifications, email, SMS text messages, and social media.

Eighty-three percent of satisfied customers are willing to refer friends and family, but only 29% do it. You can reward active customers for new referrals with discounts and prizes that range between 20-50% of what a new customer is worth, or whatever you see fit, by sending out email, SMS text, or by utilizing social media. If customers haven't reviewed your business yet, this is an opportunity to ask for testimonials. You can ask for reviews to pre-qualify them for their future reward.

You can use those reviews to brand and market your business across the web and the more your reputation grows, the more sales you will make, the more your reach will expand, and the more happy customers you will have to refer you new clients. This is how the cycle works and how you can leverage your mobile app to maximize sales and profits.

Your App Traffic Formula

In this segment, I will give you a short list of services that are often overlooked, which businesses need in their marketing. These services increase your conversion rate, help you grow your business, and put your business on the map. Most of the time, they are used separately. In this example, what we're looking for is the synergetic and compounding effect you can get when they work in unison.

I will not dive into the technicalities of each one of them for the sake of time, because there are lots of articles and books written on the topic you can research to get an education. Nevertheless, giving you an overview of this strategy will help you understand why stacking them up in your favor is a must and how their synergetic effect with your app is the icing on the cake you need to turbo-charge your business. When you follow through and implement this strategy, your competition will wonder what hit them and why your sales and traffic are soaring, and why they're trailing behind you and are having trouble catching up. These tools that I'm talking about are:

> ➢ Reputation Marketing
> ➢ Maps Marketing
> ➢ Mobile Website

Reputation Marketing

Word of mouth advertising has been around since humans were able to talk. When we want to buy a new house, a new car, or go on vacation, we always seek the council and advice of friends and family to make a good decision. What we seek most is a good experience and what we tend to avoid is bad experience. It's no different when you're buying and selling stuff on the Internet! Thanks to citation sites and social media, we live in a reputation economy, where nearly everything online is monitored and sales and deals are done solely by the sheer power of recommendation in the form of testimonials and reviews. How are books sold on Amazon? With third party recommendation, the more reviews a book has, the better because this is the kind of social proof people like to read online before making a decision. It helps tremendously!

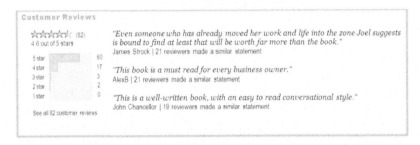

Fig. 2.7 Amazon Customer Reviews vs. No Reviews

When a book on Amazon receives a ton of critiques and reviews, this makes it much easier for a buyer to click on the "buy" button than when there's little or no information. If you ever bought a book, software, or movie online, you want to know the experience others have had before with the product you want to buy. You feel comfortable knowing you made the right choice based on those feedbacks you read. Traditional marketing platforms such as TV, radio, and print will never go out of business because of this new service; there will always be commercial breaks on your favorite TV show, but social media and citation sites have added a new twist to the game, one that was never there before.

You don't need to search the Yellow Pages if you're looking for a dentist in your local area or if you want a new pair of shoes. You go on Google or on your cell phone to get the answer! Whatever result Google returns for your search keywords, you will choose a business based on the default ranking in the search results and the number of reviews this business has. The more positive reviews and the higher the business ranks the better. You will discard businesses with little or bad reviews as you skim through the entire list to find the perfect match and I will add that at least 10 positive reviews is what it takes for a buyer to lean your way.

Fig. 2.8 Local Searches

Building a strong reputation online is the foundation. This will position you as a reputable business in your local area and a trusted name in your industry. There are many ways to do it. Reputation marketing is different than reputation management in the sense that it's the process of building a **"5-star"** reputation online and leveraging that reputation to brand your business and get more sales. Reputation management is the process of cleaning up negative reviews associated with your name and business in the search engines. Reputation marketing has an offensive posture, while reputation management has a defensive posture.

Reputation marketing is the marriage between reputation management and brand marketing. There are 4 major steps in the process: 1st) you build a reputation, 2nd) you market that reputation, 3rd) you manage that reputation and 4th) you develop a reputation culture inside your business. With client feedbacks you know exactly where weaknesses inside your business are so you can resolve them internally. You can train your staff to better respond to negative reviews, improve the quality of your service, and minimize risks of a backlash with bad publicity online. It is not unusual to fire personnel and hire new ones as a result of those bad reviews and poor results, when you know where mistakes are often made.

5-Star Reviews

Building that foundation will set you apart from businesses that have no control on what's being said about them online and can't stop bad reviews from sabotaging their business on the Internet, literally sucking out their lifeblood like leeches until they drown! You can send sporadic surveys from your app to your customers, asking them to rate your business from 1 to 10 for example, your staff, products and services, reception, etc. This will give you a glimpse and the kind of feedback you need to clean out the dirt you never saw before inside your business and provide you with solutions.

Maps Marketing
With your 5-star reviews, you can level up the playing field by dominating the local listings in your area. Businesses listed inside the 7-pack on the first page of Google get most of the traffic online and their phones are literally ringing off the hook. Some businesses dominate the local listings by default because of their geographical location — the closer you are to the center, the higher you rank — whereas others will dominate the local listings because they are feeding the kind of information Google loves.

Many factors will determine how well you rank on Google. Chief amongst them are reviews, your citations, your search keywords, your category, your backlinks, your website SEO, your website metadata, your description, coupons and special offers, your mobile website, your Google authorship status, social signals, etc. A citation is a fancy word for your business name, address, and contact information. When you've done your homework, the top spot is for grab and you will outrank your competition 99% of the time, resulting in more traffic, more phone calls, more clients, and more sales for you!

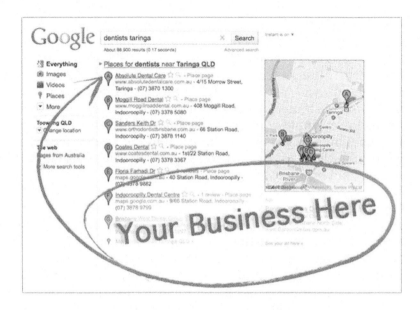

Fig. 2.9 Google Maps' 7-Pack

Mobile Website

You rank high in the local listings, you are crushing it with your raving 5-star reviews, your telephone is ringing off the hook, your website is getting a ton of traffic, but not everyone seems happy. In fact, you're losing a ton of traffic because your website is not mobile-optimized and worst of all, it has flash animation, which doesn't work with mobile devices, as we've seen it in the first chapter. What can you do? How many people are searching for your business from their mobile devices right now, only to turn to the competition because they couldn't open your website on their cell phones?

There are over 5.4 billion cell phones worldwide and this happens all the time. This is the most common problem cell phone users have, around the world. If you're using flash animation, it's even worse and you need a total redesign of your website. This may be the opportunity you've been waiting for to do a full SEO audit of your website, just so that you know how you perform online and to learn where you're potentially losing money on mobile devices and on the Internet. A SEO

142

audit solves this problem; it will help your rankings in the search engines tremendously, increase your conversion rates, and keep your bounce rate to a bare minimum. If you don't have this information, you won't know where you're losing money on the Internet and it's never too late to get a SEO audit done on your website.

Mobilegeddon, April 21st, 2015

As the years pass and the influence of technology continues to grow, the rate of Internet searches on mobile phones is constantly on the rise! Research in 2013 indicated that about 30% of Internet searches were conducted on mobile devices, with the expectation that the rate will continue to surge upwards (Source: KPCB, Internet Trends 2014). For the first time in history and not without consequences, Internet searches on mobile devices exceeded searches done on desktop computers; documented in November 2014 to be exact. In light of this Internet usage movement, six months after the aforementioned study, Google announced in April 2015 a new algorithm named Mobilegeddon to determine website ranking. The algorithm would measure the mobile-friendliness of sites and rank them accordingly; those websites not optimized for mobiles were pushed downwards and ultimately out of sight.

With this decree,[31] people had the opportunity to substantiate the compliance of their websites with mobile devices[32] and try to make the necessary changes to maintain or even surpass competitors' ranking. Google has also introduced a new icon that shows up in searches and tells users which website is mobile friendly and which one is not. Mobilegeddon penalizes businesses and bloggers around the world much harder than with previous updates such as Penguin or Panda. Google is exerting heavy pressure on business owners and bloggers either to adapt to the changes or disappear and will not content itself to expect the change arising by itself over time.

---

[31] http://googlewebmastercentral.blogspot.in/2015/04/faqs-april-21st-mobile-friendly.html
[32] https://www.google.com/webmasters/tools/mobile-friendly/?utm_source=wmc-blog&utm_medium=referral&utm_campaign=mobile-friendly

BrentDPayne (@BrentDPayne) | Twitter

»——→ ▯ https://twitter.com/**BrentDPayne**
The latest Tweets from **BrentDPayne**
(**@BrentDPayne**): "Coupons, Coupon Codes,
Promo Codes...When Content Is ...

Daily Mail

»——→ ▯ www.dailymail.co.uk/.../sex-text-mini...
22 hours ago - Tory MP **Brooks Newmark**,
pictured with his wife Lucy, said he would
quit at the general election next ...

Google Mobile Icon in Search Results

Having a mobile-optimized website like in the image above is not only essential for re-capturing the lost traffic but this will also improve your SEO dramatically as Google rewards savvy businesses and entrepreneurs with mobile websites in the local listings than those that neglect mobile users. A news hub like Daily Mail in the UK could lose a significant amount of traffic and subsequent ad money from its mobile traffic if it does not update its website fast. This update affects websites worldwide large and small regardless of authority, page views, on and off page optimization, social signals and what have you.

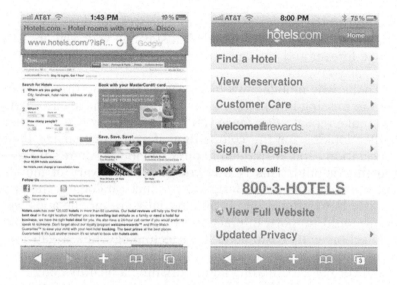

Not Optimized vs. Optimized Mobile Website

Let's recap! You have a good reputation online, you top the local listings, and your website works like a charm on desktop PCs and mobile devices. What's missing? How about a link to a mobile app? Question: Why would you need a link to an app on your mobile website? The answer is fourfold and obvious: more sales, traffic, referrals, and better customer retention!

You see, if you follow through on this app traffic formula, you will dominate your competition and crush it 99% of the time. Your telephone will be ringing off the hook and best of all you will expand your reach on mobile devices! As we know from the first chapter, a mobile website is designed to drive traffic, and there's no guarantee this traffic will come anytime soon once visitors leave your page.

This is the dilemma bloggers and businesses face all the time on the Internet. Traffic is such a precious commodity and without it, you can't do business. With this method I'm providing you with, you're maneuvering your business onto the sweet spot. Now that you understand the reason for lead capture forms on websites and mobile apps, you know why you need some devices to stay connected with visitors. A mobile app is the perfect companion for Smartphones; this is the backend you need to run your business on mobile devices 24/7. It's interactive, fun, creates value, and has more functionality to

145

respond to customers' needs. A mobile website does not have this capability. Once downloaded, it stays on your visitor's cell phone forever and you can send them offer after offer as many times as you want.

That's why mobile apps like we've seen in the first chapter are the missing link in your sales funnel to manage customers and make repeat sales. Once you land a client, why would they bother looking for the competition if you can manage their expectations and keep them happy? Obviously, there's no reason they should. This is why you should be wary of mobile website solutions that offer great product catalogues, menu à la carte buy buttons, etc. as an alternative to mobile apps, yet fail to build rapport, interact and build this loyalty, trust and connection with customers. This technology fills a gap and brings businesses and customers much closer to one another than ever before. Building and nourishing a healthy, long lasting relationship is the golden rule to running and maintaining a business successfully for long term relationship.

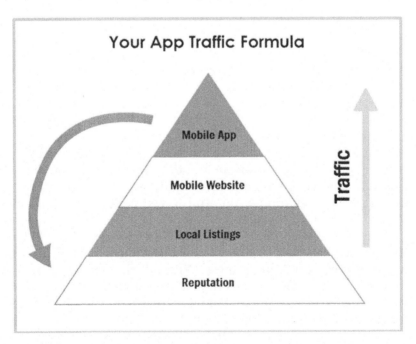

Your Mobile Marketing Blueprint

In this chapter we are going to talk about your mobile strategy going forward. This is a simple checklist of items you'll need to run your mobile marketing campaigns. From the information in the chapters above, we know how loyalty, customer retention and managing customers' expectation are important. First, your mobile marketing strategy should comprise a mobile app and a mobile optimized website.

The basic requirements for your mobile website are as follow: business contact information, an about you page, a product or service page, tap-to-call, tap-to-map, lead capture form, and social media buttons. Nowadays, these functionalities are prevalent in most WordPress responsive themes you can find on the market. We can update your current website and mobile-optimize it without a major makeover, just in case your website theme is not responsive. Please submit a ticket on page 174 to schedule a consultation with our support desk.

You will need a Facebook and Twitter account to post and send out messages to your followers and a YouTube account if you plan using video in your marketing. Having a LinkedIn account can be useful as well and these social networking sites are free to join.

2nd) Shoot for the top spot on Google, as this should be your first priority! Traffic is the lifeblood of any business, be it online or offline. Businesses downtown get a lot more foot traffic than businesses on the outskirts of metropolitan cities. Likewise, strive to rank high on Google, aim for the 7-Pack; the top 3 preferably! This is where the traffic is at on Google; not on page 2, 3 or 10; and this is where you need to be. Follow the steps outlined in the last chapter and share your website in as many website directories as you can. The more you spread your links across the web; the more you increase the likelihood of getting found in places where you least expect it. Also, hang your QR codes in and outside your business and use them inside advertisements and commercials.

3rd) Depending on the type of service you sell, you can sign up for a SMS marketing service to run your daily or weekly offers, or you can use push-notifications.

4th) When uploading your mobile app inside the app stores, always verify that your app is compliant with Apple's guidelines to be downloaded by your target audience. Please contact us if you need support to handle this process from A to Z. If you scan the QR code on the next page, you'll see live examples of real apps you can play with just to see how they work.

URL: http://previewyourapp.com

Enter these codes below inside the email field to view them, hit "next" and then press "go: **"gertlerlaw," "oandn," "ccfd1,"** and **"michigangolf."** When you scan the QR code below, you'll find an example of a mobile website with a link embedded to a downloadable app of the retail store giant Macy's.[33]

---

[33] URL: http://m.macys.com

"Get Our App"

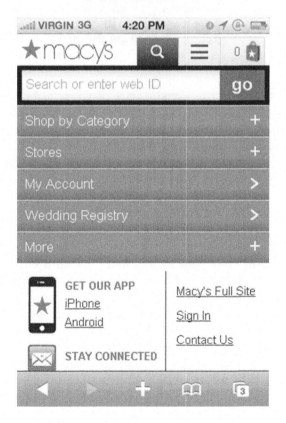

Mobile Website & Mobile App

149

Below is an example of a mobile directory for restaurants.[34]

5th) Next, when the logistic part of your mobile marketing strategy is taken care of, figure out how many downloads you need. Any app on a Smartphone is an asset working for you. People who downloaded your app want your products and services; they granted you permission to send them advertisement. Go back to the chapters where we talk about downloads and see how you can implement this strategy in your business. Please get in touch with us in case you need a marketing plan. Other simple ways to promote your app we have not discussed yet are your Facebook page. Make sure all your fans know that your app is available and entice them to download it with special offers. Also, how many emails do you send out each day? Put a link to your app at the bottom of each email signature and share it with the people you connect with the most. Ask them to tell others about it, too.

Keep your customers from drifting away by incorporating new features into your app from time to time. With each fresh idea added, take advantage of the media and issue press releases on well-known sites like PRWeb.com and other such publications in the mobile industry to raise awareness and

---

[34] URL: http://restaurantsonmobilekoeln.de

recognition. In addition, try to come up with creative ways to have your customers leave reviews for your app. One way to do that is to place incentives. For example, if you are a food business, you can offer a free sampler dish or a certain discount percentage if the customers show proof of having written a review for your app. Encourage them to rate you honestly; it will help you in the long run. Lastly, you can pick the best worded reviews and place them at the forefront of your website for prospective eyes to see at first glance.

In business terms, apps can be considered as merit goods in a sense because they are undervalued; both businesses and people do not realize the potential that apps yield with their positive externalities. Therefore, it is crucial to market your app on an exponential level because it creates a word-of-mouth stir. You will notice that your own customers will begin talking about your app and unknowingly market it. Your strategy should be as such, because many people today rely on the thoughts and opinions of their friends, family and acquaintances rather than a company's mission statement and advertisement claims.

6th) With enough downloads under your belt, your main focus should be list building. You need a list to make sales and manage customers because at this stage, your app has no commercial value if it does not put your users in a database. A list is the best asset you will ever have in your business in many respects. You can use this list to run special offers and discounts on slow days, just to fill in tables if you're a business that relies heavily on volume and traffic. You want to boost sales and remind customers to visit you regularly? This is how you do it, for a better reinforcement of your customer and to keep them consistently coming back to you. Other sales tools at your disposal are push-notifications and SMS text messages.

7th) When should you run coupons, special offers and discounts, and how often, this is entirely up to you. You can run contests and give stuff away for free and use your app to create some buzz in your community. Be creative; use your app to stage events for promotions and product launches too! Please get in touch with us for a consultation about the options that are available to you from your mobile business application. Please submit a ticket to our support desk at: support [at] appsolutemarketingx.com.

8th) Use your app for customer satisfaction surveys and market research. The possibilities are endless; you're just one click away from that little piece of information that can give you the extra edge. You can drill down the information to a subatomic level with multiple questions, drop down menus, check boxes and forms pointing at image galleries, charts and even video files. You have the best data collection tool on the planet, bar none for market research, none of the best market research firms can rival with!

9th) Speed of implementation in the digital space is everything. If you find yourself in a situation where you are competing with businesses with similar products, prices, services, etc., your app could be a tiebreaker for many reasons as we have seen. Do not wait for the competition to gain the upper-hand in cyberspace. At this stage you want to be on top of your game when there's little or no competition. Bear in mind that on average, people save 63 apps on their cell phones, and their attention span is very short. This is why sharing your app very quickly in a very competitive environment has its merits. Follow this simple blueprint and you shouldn't have any problem running a successful campaign. The future is yours and it's mobile!

Final Note

We have reached the conclusion of this book. I hope you have enjoyed reading it and that you have learned something new about apps and mobile marketing. I have listed the basic functionalities you can find inside a mobile app business; however, you have the option of 30 more functionalities.

As technology continues to evolve, you will be updated with the new changes. The app industry is only 7 years old; it's still in its infancy, and has great years ahead of itself. I can't wait to see what the future holds for this very young and dynamic industry and how it will impact businesses in terms of sales and lead generation.

This new technology allows businesses to connect one-on-one with customers on a much deeper level than ever before, with text, sound, images and video. Mobile apps are the new game in town, they have become the eyes and ears of the market, and we are barely scratching the surface of its potential. Where it will take us, only the future will tell. When you decide to host your app inside the app stores, there are many things you need to consider. Not every app is accepted instantly inside the Apple store; in fact, quite the opposite.

There are a series of guidelines your app needs to fulfill to be downloaded by your target audience. Apple values quality apps that offer a great user experience, great functionality, and top notch graphic designs. Not many app developers and businesses are aware of this, which explains why most applications inside the Apple store result in rejections 30% of the time. You are well advised to seek the guidance of a consultant, who will help you position your business before this great opportunity.

Our knowledge and expertise encompasses a wide range of fields such as app marketing, app design & development, mobile marketing, social media, Internet marketing, and much more. You are welcome to contact us at any time. If you have questions, thoughts, and ideas regarding apps, or other topics of interest, please feel free to submit a ticket to our support desk at: support [at] appsolutemarketingx.com and we will be glad to assist you. Also, if you have friends and colleagues you know can benefit from this information, you are welcome to refer them kindly to this book. On this note, thanks again for reading; it was a pleasure writing this book for you! I hope you enjoyed it and I wish you all the best in your marketing endeavors for 2015 and beyond.

Sincerely,
Maurice Ufituwe

One Last Thing

Thanks for reading! If you enjoyed this book or found it useful, I'd be very grateful if you could post a short review on Amazon. Your support really does make a difference and I read all the reviews I get personally so I can make changes and improve this book even more. If you'd like to leave a short review, all you have to do is scan the QR code below to share your testimonial on this book here:

URL: http://amzn.to/YeJAEb

Also, don't forget to share it with friends and family! Chose one of your preferred networking site on the order page, click the icon and you'll be able to share across the Internet.

Enter a promotion code or Gift Card

Share

Thanks again for your support!

Follow Us & Contact Information

If you like this book, please like us and follow us on Facebook, YouTube, Twitter, and Pinterest! We will update you with special offers, tips, information, and industry news as we get them when you follow us. Thanks in advance.

Facebook:
https://www.facebook.com/AppMarketingX

YouTube:
https://www.youtube.com/c/AppMarketingX

Twitter:
https://twitter.com/AppMarketingX

Pinterest:
https://pinterest.com/AppMarketingX

Instagram:
https://instagram.com/AppMarketingX

Special LinkedIn Group

Come join our LinkedIn Group just for readers like you who want to take their marketing to the next level. In this group, we will share our success stories, marketing tips, and strategies so we can all benefit and continue to grow our businesses together. This is also a fantastic group for finding joint venture partners and cross promotion opportunities! Imagine if you had hundreds of other entrepreneurs from all over the world collaborating with you — imagine how big of an impact you could have. It's also a great place to get any marketing questions you have answered as well.

"Come join us today on LinkedIn!"

LinkedIn: http://www.linkedin.com/groups/Join-Now-If-You-Want-4754690

Contact information:
If you're serious about increasing sales and would like to schedule a free consultation to see how we can set a comprehensive marketing campaign for your business, please feel free to contact us by leaving your name, telephone and email address at the telephone number at this URL: http://www.appsolutemarketingx.com. We will gladly assist you.

How to Get an iPhone for Free

Are you one of the people who've dreamed of an iPhone, iPad, or Android, and couldn't afford one? Would you like to get your hands on your first Smartphone without paying a red cent? Maybe you think this is not possible?

Rest assured, this is not an April fool's joke and it's not a gimmick either. Far from that, and yes, this is for real. You can get your first iPhone shipped to your home within days simply by registering to this website: **http://oozof.com/YHWMhj** and by referring friends and family to this website. Once you've done this, that's it, there's nothing else you need to do! Copy and paste this URL inside your browser or scan the QR code below to register to the website.

To get an iPhone or an iPad, you need to earn credits. For example, you'll need 50 credits for an iPhone and 29 credits to get an iPad. The more people you refer to this site, the more credits you will earn. If you don't want an iPhone or iPad, there are other brands to choose from like Nokia, Blackberry, etc., or you can get MP3 Players, HDTVs, gaming consoles, or Kindle devices sent to you if you want. How's that for a start? There's more than just an iPhone in store and you decide what device you want to get!

URL: http://oozof.com/YHWMhj

Enjoy!

Are You Getting the Attention that You Deserve?

Don't go there, we are here!...

Are you getting the attention you want? How many customers can find your business online? Many businesses know that the Internet and mobile is the future, but have no idea how to make good use of them and/or how to attract customers inside their business.

There is a plethora of tools businesses can take advantage of to get the kind of attention they want online, but they don't utilize them for lack of knowledge. From Google maps to social media, mobile websites, reputation marketing, and lots in between, many of these tools go unnoticed and yet can increase sales dramatically. Learn new ways of multiplying your sources of income on the Internet and mobile devices today!

Landing Customers in the App Stores

Are you an app developer or a business owner trying to land clients in the app stores? Do you know what it takes to get clicks, and get clients excited in your app? If ranking a website on Google is a challenge, ranking your app inside the app stores is a daunting task. You need downloads? We can help! For more information, please send us an email for support: appsolutemarketingx.com. We'll be glad to help you out.

http://appsolutemarketingx.com

Google Maps

Is your business visible on Google, or is your competition getting all the attention and sales you deserve? Only the top 7 businesses listed on Google Maps get most of the traffic and rewards on page one of Google Maps; their telephone is literally ringing off the hook! Also, can customers access your website from their cell phones or do they seek out your competition out of frustration?

This is a key ranking factor on Google Maps! Businesses not visible on Google are a shadow of themselves and those that lack a mobile website have simply given up hope on making sales on mobile devices. For more information on how we can land you clients with Google Maps, please send us an email for support: moremobilemarketingx.com, we'll be glad to help you out.

http://moremobilemarketingx.com

Landing Clients with 5-Star Reviews

Easy access to information gives people the power to vote with their dollars online. Imagine you've arrived in Milan, Italy on a 2-week trip and you're shopping around for the best pizzas. You grab your Smartphone, punch in a few keywords and Google gives you results based on your location and the best recommendations. You skim through the list hunting for the best deals. Not knowing the place, you pick the restaurant with the top reviews.

Now on the flipside, imagine you are one of those pizza shops with 1 or 2 bad reviews. You just lost one client there! How many businesses are losing money this way? Do you see the power of reviews? How do you get raving reviews and how do you stop bad ones from sabotaging your business? For more information on how to market businesses with reviews, please send us an email for support: webbrandsreputationmarketing.com, we'll be glad to help you out.

http://webbrandsreputationmarketing.com

Mobile Websites

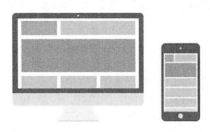

Google has implemented a new algorithm which has taken effect since April 21st, 2015. That's the biggest update since the Penguin and Panda updates to affect millions and billions of websites, blogs, E-commerce platforms and Web 2.0 web properties around the world. The algorithm measures the mobile-friendliness of sites and ranks them accordingly.

Those websites not optimized for mobile are pushed downwards and ultimately out of sight, meaning subsequent loss of traffic and money unless nothing is done to reverse the situation. How safe are you from the penalties and what can you do to protect your web properties from the coming onslaught? To learn how you can update your website effectively with minimal effort, call us today or send us an email for support: moremobilemarketingx.com. We'll be glad to help you out!

http://moremobilemarketingx.com

Augmented Reality

Augmented Reality or AR in short is a technology that super-imposes a computer-generated image on a user's view of the real world from a handheld device, thus providing a composite view. This technology has multiple applications in commerce, science, industry, marketing and entertainment.

People can remotely access business information such as products and services sold, prices, etc., simply by pointing their mobile devices towards your business, regardless of the distance they find themselves at in space. For more information about the marketing options that are available to you, please send us an email for support: moremobilemarketingx.com, we'll be glad to help you out.

http://moremobilemarketingx.com

Local Lead Generation System

How would you like to get exclusive phone leads calling to do business with you today? Are you looking for a sales representative who can land you clients on a commission basis? Because you see, we get paid when you get paid! With our proprietary system most sales, most appointments and deals are set up over the phone. We take care of everything!

We will build you a responsive website for your business designed to land you clients. We will fire up our leads generating system; we will get your phone ringing, and you'll pay us when the phone actually starts ringing. Interested? For more information on how we can help, please send us an email for support: moremobilemarketingx.com, we'll be glad to help you out.

http://moremobilemarketingx.com

TV and Billboard Ads

Would you like to run a 30 sec. ad on your favorite TV show for a fraction of what major advertising companies charge for it? Would you like to have your business featured on the most trafficked highways in the US? This is your chance to make an impact, and increase sales with a high return for less.

Advertising for pennies on national TV and on billboards is actually possible with the right connections! Let us expand your reach nationwide across the US starting today! For more information on how to run ads on TV and billboards for less, please send us an email for support: moremobilemarketingx.com, we'll be glad to help you out. (This offer is currently available in the US.)

http://moremobilemarketingx.com

Social Media

Is social media part of your sales channel or do you regard it as a passing fad for teenagers that plainly doesn't work? There are millions of people on Facebook; this is the biggest social media website on the planet. YouTube is the 2nd largest search engine of the world after Google, and is by definition a social networking site. If you add Twitter and Instagram to the mix, you have huge hives of interconnected people in cyberspace waiting to be harvested like fish boats casting their nets over billions of fish in deep sea. Also, contrary to popular belief, social media sells! For more information on how you can drive sales with social media, please send us an email for support: socialmediamarketingx.com, we'll be glad to help you out.

http://socialmediamarketingx.com

Got an App Idea?

You've been dallying for a while with the idea of creating your first app and didn't know how to do it. You got an awesome super cool idea for an app; an idea that you know will be a major hit; the idea you know that will storm the charts and transform the face of the world. You've heard countless success stories from rags to riches, of businesses and individuals who've made it with thousands and millions of downloads, know deeply in your heart that apps are the next big thing! Yet you lack the resources to transform your idea into a reality, you simply don't know where to start.

If this is your case, tell us more about your super idea, and let us take you by the hand. We've got the development and marketing resources you need to succeed in the app stores; we'll turn your dreams into a reality! Call us today or send us an email for support: ecommercemauricevictor.com, we'll be glad to help you out!

http://ecommercemauricevictor.com

Schedule a Meeting with Us

Would you like to develop your Mobile app, run your app campaign, maybe you want more visibility and exposure via Google Maps, Social Media and a mobile website? Please scan the QR code[35] below by providing us with your business contact information, the service you're interested in and the best time to reach out to you. We look forward to assisting you.

---

[35] URL: http://oozof.com/BVpQfO

Broadcast This Information

How many businesses in your local area are mobile savvy and of these businesses, how many do you know have successfully implemented a mobile marketing strategy? Do you know a friend or a colleague who needs help? If so, please spread the word, share this knowledge and hand them a copy of this book. They will reward you tenfold for taking action!

Impress friends and family; teach them how to sell with **Mobile Apps!** Order more Copies here:

Glossary

3D: The quality of being three-dimensional or A three-dimensional medium, display, or performance, such as a cinematic or graphic medium in three dimensions.

Ad blindness: Ad blindness is a term used to denote the state of conscious or subconscious ignorance of advertisements placed on a webpage by visitors due to various reasons like irrelevance, vanilla design and familiarization of the webpage layout.

Ad placements: Locations throughout the Content Network where your ad can appear.

Add-on services: An add-on service in business and commerce is a feature that can be added to a standard model or package to give increased benefits.

Algorithm: A process or set of rules to be followed in calculations or other problem-solving operations, especially by a computer. In the case of websites, it is usually instituted by search engine requirements for ranking a website.

App: A self-contained program or piece of software designed to fulfill a particular purpose; an application, especially as downloaded by a user to a mobile device.

App agencies: Companies or businesses involved in the process of selling and marketing mobile apps on mobile devices.

App description: Text describing the usage and functionality of the app.

App store: The App Store is a service for the iPhone, iPod Touch and iPad created by Apple Inc. which allows users to browse and download applications from the iTunes Store that were developed with the iPhone SDK and published through Apple.

Apps: Plural of app

Banner ads: A web banner or banner ad is a form of advertising on the World Wide Web. This form of online advertising entails embedding an advertisement into a webpage. It is intended to attract traffic to a website by linking to the website of the advertiser to the banner.

Blog: A personal website or webpage, on which an individual records opinions, links to other sites, etc. on a regular basis.

Blogger: A person who keeps and updates a blog.

Blogosphere: personal websites and blogs collectively.

Business app: "Business app" or business application refers to any mobile application that is important to running your business.

Camera: A device for recording visual images in the form of photographs, movie film, or video signals.

Cash-flow: The total amount of money being transferred into and out of a business, especially as affecting liquidity.

Cell phone: Short for "cellular phone." A cellular phone is a telephone with access to a cellular radio system so it can be used over a wide area, without a physical connection to a network.

Citation management system: A citation management system is a proactive process inside a business that utilizes an interface to garner customers' feedback and testimonials on the Internet. The advantage of this type of review collection system is that it spares your clients the time and hassle of searching your business on review sites to rate it online. It allows you to filter good reviews from bad reviews you can utilize to market your business and address grievances when they arise. This system allows you to spot and weed out weaknesses inside your organization and avoids negative comments from landing on citation sites to tarnish your reputation online.

Citation sites: Citation sites are websites that keep record of business contact information across the web and where customers can leave personal experiences and recommendations to other visitors about your business (see review sites).

Comment capture page: A comment capture page inside a citation management system is a page used to garner customers' feedback and testimonials.

Conversion rate: Conversion rate in Internet marketing is the ratio of visitors who convert casual content views or website visits into desired actions based on subtle or direct requests from marketers, advertisers, and content creators.

Credit card: A small plastic card issued by a bank, business, etc., allowing the holder to purchase goods or services on credit.

CRM: Short for "Customer Relationship Management" is a model for managing a company's interactions with current and future customers. It involves using technology to organize, automate, and synchronize sales, marketing, customer service, and technical support.

Cross-sell: Sell a different product or service to an existing customer.

Custom data capture form: See "opt-in form."

Customer attrition: Customer attrition, also known as customer churn, customer turnover, or customer defection, is the loss of clients or customers.

Customer loyalty: The loyalty business model is a business model used in strategic management in which company resources are employed so as to increase the loyalty of customers and other stakeholders in the expectation that corporate objectives will be met or surpassed.

Customer relationship management: See CRM

Customer rewards programs: Customer rewards programs, also known as loyalty programs, are reward programs offered by a company to customers who frequently make purchases. A loyalty program may give a customer advanced access to new products, special sales coupons or free merchandise. Customers typically register their personal information with the company and are given a unique identifier, such as a numerical ID or membership card, and use that identifier when making a purchase.

Desktop PCs: A desktop computer is a personal computer (PC) in a form intended for regular use at a single location, as opposed to a mobile laptop or portable computer. Prior to the widespread use of microprocessors, a computer that could fit on a desk was considered remarkably small.

Digital Marketing: Digital marketing is the promoting of brands using all forms of digital advertising. This now includes Television, Radio, Internet, mobile and any other form of digital media.

Digital Space: The digital space encompasses technologies and innovations within computation, data transfer, and data-enabled devices. The most direct examples being your computer, the Internet, and mobile phones. Beyond technological innovation, the digital space includes social innovation surrounding the adoption of digital technologies.

Direct Marketing: The business of selling products or services directly to the public, e.g. by mail order or telephone selling, rather than through retailers.

Discount: A deduction from the usual cost of something, typically given for prompt or advance payment, use of a coupon or to a special category of buyers.

180

DUI: Driving under the influence (DUI) commonly called "drunk driving," it refers to operating a motor vehicle while one's blood alcohol content is above the legal limit set by statute, which supposedly is the level at which a person cannot drive safely. In the U.S. this rate is set at .08 percent.

E-commerce: Commercial transactions conducted electronically on the Internet.

Edge rank: *EdgeRank* is an algorithm developed by Facebook to govern what is displayed and how high on the News Feed.

Email auto-responder: When a customer sends an e-mail to a certain address manned by an auto responder, this powerful mailbot automatically fires back an email response, usually an informative sales letter. Auto responders are the email equivalent of a fax-back service.

Email campaign: Building and sending an email, or series of emails with a common theme, to your recipients. A campaign can be a newsletter or consist of other offers.

Email list: An electronic mailing list is a special usage of email that allows for widespread distribution of information to many Internet users.

Email marketing: E-mail marketing is a form of direct marketing which uses electronic mail as a means of communicating commercial or fundraising messages to an audience. In its broadest sense, every e-mail sent to a potential or current customer could be considered e-mail marketing.

Engagement marketing: Engagement marketing, sometimes called "experiential marketing," "event marketing," "live marketing," or "participation marketing," is a marketing strategy that directly engages consumers and invites and encourages consumers to participate in the evolution of a brand.

Facebook application: The Facebook Platform provides a set of APIs and tools which enable 3rd party developers to integrate with the "open graph" — whether through applications on Facebook.com or external websites and devices.

Fan base: The fans of a sports team, pop music group, etc., considered as a distinct social grouping.

Fan page: A Fan page within Facebook is a page that you set up to promote your company, blog, product, etc. Surfers can become fans of the page and thereby be updated when you make posts to your wall.

Flash animation: A Flash animation or Flash cartoon is an animated film which is created using Adobe Flash or similar animation software and often distributed in the .swf file format.

Foot traffic: Pedestrian traffic; people coming and going on foot.

Functionality: The range of operations that can be run on a computer or other electronic system.

Geo-fencing: Geo-fencing is a feature in a software program that uses the global positioning system (GPS) or radio frequency identification (RFID) to define geographical boundaries. A geo-fence is a virtual barrier. Programs that incorporate geo-fencing allow an administrator to set up triggers so when a device enters (or exits) the boundaries defined by the administrator, a text message or email alert is sent. Many geo-fencing applications incorporate Google Earth, allowing administrators to define boundaries on top of a satellite view of a specific geographical area. Other applications define boundaries by longitude and latitude or through user-created and Web-based maps.

Gold rush: A rapid movement of people to a newly discovered gold field. The first major gold rush, to California in 1848–49, was followed by others in the US, Australia (1851–53), South Africa (1884), and Canada (Klondike, 1897–98).

182

GPS function: The Global Positioning System (GPS) is a space-based satellite navigation system that provides location and time information in all weather conditions, anywhere on or near the Earth where there is an unobstructed line of sight to four or more GPS satellites. The system provides critical capabilities to military, civil and commercial users around the world. It is maintained by the United States government and is freely accessible to anyone with a GPS receiver.

Great Depression: The Great Depression was a severe worldwide economic depression in the decade preceding World War II. The timing of the Great Depression varied across nations, but in most countries it started in 1930 and lasted until the late 1930s or middle 1940s. It was the longest, most widespread, and deepest depression of the 20th century.

Groupon: Groupon is a deal-of-the-day website that is localized to major markets in the United States and Canada. The first market for Groupon was Chicago, followed soon thereafter by Boston and New York City and Toronto. Groupon serves more than 40 markets and was launched in November 2008.

Hashtag: A Hashtag on social media sites such as Twitter is a word or phrase preceded by a hash or pound sign (#) and used to identify messages on a specific topic.

Icon: A person or thing regarded as a representative symbol of something.

Incentivized survey: A paid or incentivized survey is a type of statistical survey where the participant/member is rewarded through an incentive program, generally entry into a sweepstakes program or a small cash reward, for completing one or more surveys.

Internet: A computer network consisting of a worldwide network of computer networks that use the TCP/IP network protocols to facilitate data transmission and exchange.

Interruption marketing: Marketing communications that disrupt customers' activities.

183

iPad: The iPad is a tablet computer designed and developed by Apple. It is particularly marketed as a platform for audio and visual media such as books, periodicals, movies, music, and games, as well as web content.

iPhone: The iPhone is a line of Internet and multimedia-enabled Smartphones designed and marketed by Apple Inc. The first iPhone was introduced on January 9, 2007.

Karaoke: A form of entertainment, offered typically by bars and clubs, in which people take turns singing popular songs into a microphone over prerecorded backing tracks.

Key performance indicator: key performance indicator (KPI) is a type of performance measurement. KPIs evaluate the success of an organization or of a particular activity in which it engages. Often success is simply the repeated, periodic achievement of some levels of operational goal (e.g. zero defects, 10/10 customer satisfaction, etc.), and sometimes success is defined in terms of making progress toward strategic goals.

Lifetime value: In marketing, customer lifetime value (CLV), lifetime customer value (LCV), or lifetime value (LTV) and a new concept of "customer life cycle management" is the present value of the future cash flows attributed to the customer relationship.

Facebook Like: The Facebook *"Like"* button is a feature that allows users to show their support for specific comments, pictures, wall posts, statuses, or fan pages. Added in February 2009, the "Like" button allows users to show their appreciation for content without having to make a written comment. While pages originally gave users the option to "become a fan" of them, Facebook replaced this option with a "Like" button in April 2010.

Local search: Local search is the use of specialized Internet search engines that allow users to submit geographically constrained searches against a structured database of local business listings. Typical local search queries include not only

184

information about "what" the site visitor is searching for (such as keywords, a business category, or the name of a consumer product) but also "where" information, such as a street address, city name, postal code, or geographic coordinates like latitude and longitude. Examples of local searches include "Hong Kong hotels," "Manhattan restaurants," and "Dublin Hertz." Local searches exhibit explicit or implicit local intent.

Loyalty program: See Customer Loyalty.

Mac: A type of personal computer developed by Apple Inc.

Market intelligence: Market intelligence (MI) is the information relevant to a company's markets, gathered and analyzed specifically for the purpose of accurate and confident decision-making in determining market opportunity, market penetration strategy, and market development metrics.

Mobile app: Short for Mobile application is a software application developed for hand held devices such as personal digital assistants, enterprise digital assistants or mobile phones.

Mobile device: A mobile device, also known as a handheld device, handheld computer or simply handheld is a pocket-sized computing device, typically having a display screen with touch input and/or a miniature keyboard.

Mobile directory: A mobile directory is a collection of subscriber details of a mobile phone operator. Generally, the mobile telephony operators do not publish a mobile directory. Some third party websites offer mobile directory facility through reverse search.

Mobile phones: Another term for a cellular phone.

Mobile website: A mobile website is the mobile version of traditional websites developed for Smartphone, tablets and hand-held devices.

Offline marketing: Methods of marketing that do not involve the internet. Examples include direct mail, billboards, and print advertising, also referred to as traditional advertising.

One-time offer: A one-time-offer page (or OTO) is a technique widely used in Internet Marketing to up-sell products and services.

Open rate: An open rate in Internet marketing is the percentage of emails and text messages that get opened for the total amount of emails and text messages sent.

Opt-in form: A form filled out by a person to receive communication from a specific website.

Pareto law: The Pareto principle (also known as the 80–20 rule, the law of the vital few, and the principle of factor scarcity) states that, for many events, roughly 80% of the effects come from 20% of the causes.

PC: A personal computer (PC) is a general-purpose computer, whose size, capabilities, and original sale price makes it useful for individuals, and which is intended to be operated directly by an end-user with no intervening computer operator.

PDF: A file format that provides an electronic image of text or text and graphics that looks like a printed document and can be viewed, printed, and electronically transmitted.

Permission marketing: Permission marketing is a term coined by Seth Godin used in marketing in general and e-marketing specifically. The undesirable opposite of permission marketing is interruption marketing. Marketers obtain permission before advancing to the next step in the purchasing process.

Podcast: A multimedia digital file made available on the Internet for downloading to a portable media player, computer, etc.

Portable device: A mobile device, also known as a handheld device, handheld computer or simply handheld is a pocket-sized computing device, typically having a display screen with touch input and/or a miniature keyboard.

Push-notification: Push-notifications are messages that are sent to users who have opted in to receive them. Different from Eblasts, the Push Notifications are small message alerts about specials sent to mobile applications.

QR code: A machine-readable code consisting of an array of black and white squares, typically used for storing URLs or other information for reading by the camera on a Smartphones.

QR coupon: QR coupons are coupon offers embedded in a QR code.

Reputation culture: A reputation culture inside a business is a systematic process designed to garner feedbacks and testimonials of customers to build a positive reputation around the business, to render better products and services and improve the perceived image and brand of the business.

Reputation management: Reputation management is the process of tracking an entity's actions and other entities' opinions about those actions; reporting on those actions and opinions; and reacting to that report creating a feedback loop. All entities involved are generally people, but that need not always be the case.

Reputation marketing: The reputation marketing field has evolved from the marriage of the fields of reputation management and brand marketing. In the socially connected world of the new millennium a brand's reputation is vetted online nearly in real-time by consumers leaving online reviews and citing experiences on social media websites.

Review site: A review site is a website on which reviews can be posted about people, businesses, products, or services. These sites may use Web 2.0 techniques to gather reviews from site users or may employ professional writers to author reviews on the topic of concern for the site.

Richard Koch: Koch, Richard (born 1950) is a former management consultant, entrepreneur, and writer of several books on how to apply the Pareto principle (80/20 rule) in all walks of life. Koch has also used his concepts to make a fortune from several private equity investments made personally.

Rich Media: A Rich Media ad contains images or video and involves some kind of user interaction. The initial load of a Rich Media ad is 40K or more. While text ads sell with words, and display ads sell with pictures, Rich Media ads offer more ways to involve an audience with an ad. The ad can expand, float, peel down, etc. And you can access aggregated metrics on your audience's behavior, including number of expansions, multiple exits, and video completions. Rich Media lets agencies create complex ads that can elicit strong user response. Using Flash or HTML5 technology, the ads can include multiple levels of content in one placement: videos, games, tweets from an ad, etc. If you have a simple objective to generate clicks or a more ambitious goal to create brand awareness, Rich Media is the format to go with.

Router: A router is a device that forwards data packets between computer networks, creating an overlay internetwork. A router is connected to two or more data lines from different networks. When a data packet comes in one of the lines, the router reads the address information in the packet to determine its ultimate destination. Then, using information in its routing table or routing policy, it directs the packet to the next network on its journey.

RSS Feed: RSS, most commonly expanded as Really Simple Syndication is a family of web feed formats used to publish frequently updated works—such as blog entries, news headlines, audio, and video—in a standardized format.

Sales funnel: A Sales tunnel, also called a Sales pipeline, or a Sales funnel to emphasize the volumetric changes in deals is the way that both direct sales persons and SFA systems visualize the sales process of a company.

Search engine: A program for the retrieval of data from a database or network, especially the Internet.

SEO: Search engine optimization (SEO) is the process of affecting the visibility of a website or a web page in a search engine's "natural" or un-paid ("organic") search results. In general, the earlier (or higher ranked on the search results page), and more frequently a site appears in the search results list, the more visitors it will receive from the search engine's users. SEO may target different kinds of search, including image search, local search, video search, academic search, news search and industry-specific vertical search engines.

SEO-optimized: Is another word for Keyword Optimization.

Shopping cart: A shopping cart is a piece of software that acts as an online store's catalog and ordering process. Typically, a shopping cart is the interface between a company's Website and its deeper infrastructure, allowing consumers to select merchandise; review what they have selected; make necessary modifications or additions; and purchase the merchandise.

Smartphone: A cellular phone that is able to perform many of the functions of a computer, typically having a relatively large screen and an operating system capable of running general-purpose applications.

SMS: Short for Short Message Service, is a text messaging service component of phone, web, or mobile communication systems. It uses standardized communications protocols to allow fixed line or mobile phone devices to exchange short text messages.

Social media: Websites and applications used for social networking.

Social networking sites: See social media.

Social networks: See social media.

Software: The programs and other operating information used by a computer.

Software applications: Application software, also known as an application, is computer software designed to help the user to perform singular or multiple related specific tasks. Examples include enterprise software, accounting software, office suites, graphics software, and media players.

Steroids: Any of a large class of organic compounds with a characteristic molecular structure containing four rings of carbon atoms (three six-membered and one five). They include many hormones, alkaloids, and vitamins.

Survey: A general view, examination, or description of someone or something.

Tablet: A tablet computer, or simply tablet, is a mobile computer with display, circuitry and battery in a single unit. Tablets are often equipped with sensors, including cameras, microphone, accelerometer and touchscreen, with finger or stylus gestures replacing computer mouse and keyboard.

Tamagotchi: An electronic toy displaying a digital image of a creature, which has to be looked after and responded to by the "owner" as if it were a real pet.

Tap-to-call: Also known as click-to-talk, click-to-chat and click-to-text, is a form of Web-based communication in which a person clicks an object (e.g., button, image or text) to request an immediate connection with another person in real-time either by phone call, Voice-over-Internet-Protocol (VoIP), or text.

Tap-to-map: Similar as tap-to-call only that the button or image you click is linked to a local map.

Technology: The application of scientific knowledge for practical purposes, esp. in industry

The 80/20 Principle: The Pareto principle (also known as the 80-20 rule, The Pareto principle has several name variations, including: Pareto's Law, the 80/20 rule, the 80:20 rule, and 80 20 rule.

Tip calculator: A device that calculates the amount of money customers will tip to a waiter, bar or restaurant.

Traffic: Website traffic is simply the amount of people that comes to visit a website, the number of pages visitors click, and the amount of time a visitor views a page on a website.

Travel Channel: A cable channel network that shows mostly travel related programming.

Tweet: A posting made on the social networking site Twitter.

Unique selling proposition: The unique selling proposition (USP), or unique selling point, or "unique selling product" or "unique selling price" is a marketing concept first proposed as a theory to explain a pattern in successful advertising campaigns of the early 1940s. The USP states that such campaigns made unique propositions to the customer that convinced them to switch brands. The term was developed by television advertising pioneer Rosser Reeves of Ted Bates & Company.

Up-sell: (Upsell) Upselling (sometimes 'up-selling') is a sales technique whereby a salesperson induces the customer to purchase more expensive items, upgrades, or other add-ons in an attempt to make a more profitable sale.

Viral image: Viral images are images that go viral on the Internet because they receive many shares, comments and "likes."

Viral message: Viral messages are messages that go viral on the Internet because they receive many shares, comments and "likes."

Voice recorder: A dictation machine is a sound recording device most commonly used to record speech for later play-back or to be typed into print. It includes digital voice recorders and tape recorders.

Web: The Web is a subset of the Internet; it is made up of pages that can be opened through the use of a Web browser.

Website: A location connected to the Internet that maintains one or more pages on the World Wide Web.

Yellow Pages: A telephone directory, or a section of one, printed on yellow paper and listing businesses and other or-ganizations according to the goods or services they offer.

List of Products and Services

Amazon

Amazon.com, Inc. is an American international multibillion dollar electronic commerce company with headquarters in Seattle, Washington, United States. It is the world's largest online retailer.

URL: http://www.amazon.com/

Android

Android is a Linux-based operating system designed primarily for touchscreen mobile devices such as Smartphones and tablet computers. Initially developed by Android, Inc., whom Google financially backed and later purchased in 2005, Android was unveiled in 2007 along with the founding of the Open Handset Alliance: a consortium of hardware, software, and telecommunication companies devoted to advancing open standards for mobile devices. The first Android-powered phone was sold in October 2008.

URL: http://www.android.com/

Apple

Apple Inc., formerly Apple Computer, Inc., is an American multinational corporation headquartered in Cupertino, California that designs, develops, and sells consumer electronics, computer software, and personal computers. Its best known hardware products are the Mac line of computers, the iPod, the iPhone, and the iPad. Its software includes the OS X and iOS operating systems, the iTunes media browser, the Safari web browser, and the iLife and iWork creativity and production suites. The company was founded on April 1, 1976, and incorporated on January 3, 1977. The word "Computer" was removed from its name on January 9, 2007, reflecting its shifted focus toward consumer electronics after the introduction of the iPhone.

URL: http://www.apple.com/

Apple App Store

The Apple App Store is a digital application distribution platform for iOS, developed and maintained by Apple Inc. The service allows users to browse and download applications that were developed with Apple's iOS SDK. The apps can be downloaded directly to an iOS device, or onto a personal computer via iTunes.

URL: https://itunes.apple.com/en/genre/ios/id36?mt=8

BlackBerry

BlackBerry Limited, formerly known as Research In Motion Limited, is a Canadian telecommunication and wireless equipment company best known as the developer of the BlackBerry brand of Smartphones and tablets.

URL: http://us.blackberry.com/

BlackBerry App World

BlackBerry World (previously BlackBerry App World) is an application distribution service and application by BlackBerry Ltd, for a majority of BlackBerry devices. The service provides BlackBerry users with an environment to browse, download, and update third-party applications.

URL:
http://appworld.blackberry.com/webstore/?%3fcountrycode
=TR&lang=en

Booshaka.com

Booshaka.com shows you what's trending on Facebook and aims to show the freshest, most relevant posts across the social web. People use Booshaka.com to find out what people on Facebook are chattering about.

URL: http://www.booshaka.com/

Buddy Media

Buddy Media, Inc. is a privately held company founded by CEO, chairman, and serial entrepreneur, Michael Lazerow, which offers some of the world's largest brands social media solutions.

Cisco

Cisco Systems, Inc. is an American multinational corporation headquartered in San Jose, California, that designs, manufactures, and sells networking equipment.
URL: http://www.cisco.com/

Exact Target

ExactTarget, now called Salesforce Marketing Cloud, is a provider of digital marketing automation and analytics software and services. It was founded in 2000.
URL: http://www.exacttarget.com/

Facebook

Facebook is a social networking service launched in February 2004, owned and operated by Facebook, Inc. As of September 2012, Facebook has over one billion active users, more than half of them using Facebook on a mobile device. Users must register before using the site, after which they may create a personal profile, add other users as friends, and exchange messages, including automatic notifications when they update their profile. Additionally, users may join common-interest user groups, organized by workplace, school or college, or other characteristics, and categorize their friends into lists such as "People From Work" or "Close Friends."
URL: http://www.facebook.com/

FourSquare

Foursquare is a location-based social networking website for mobile devices, such as Smartphones. Users "check in" at venues using a mobile website, text messaging, or a device-specific application by selecting from a list of venues the application locates nearby. Location is based on GPS hardware in the mobile device or network location provided by the application. Each check-in awards the user points and sometimes "badges."
URL: https://foursquare.com/

Gartner

Gartner, Inc. is an American information technology research and advisory firm headquartered in Stamford,

Connecticut, United States. It was known as Gartner Group until 2001
URL: http://www.gartner.com/technology/home.jsp

Google
Google, Inc. is an American multinational corporation specializing in Internet-related services and products. These include search, cloud computing, software, and online advertising technologies. Most of its profits are derived from AdWords.
URL: https://www.google.com/

Hashtags.org
Hashtags.org is a service that provides real-time tracking of Twitter hashtags without the necessity of following a specific Twitter account.
URL: http://www.hashtags.org/

LinkedIn
LinkedIn is a social networking website founded in December, 2002, for people in professional occupations and is mainly used for professional networking. As of June, 2013, LinkedIn reports more than 225 million acquired users in more than 200 countries and territories.
URL: http://www.linkedin.com/

Mashable
Mashable (Mashable Inc.) is a Scottish-American news website and Internet news blog founded by Pete Cashmore. The website's primary focus is social media news but also covers news and developments in mobile, entertainment, online video, business, web development, technology, memes, and gadgets. Mashable was launched by Pete Cashmore from his home in Aberdeen, Scotland in July 2005. With a reported 50+ million monthly page views and an Alexa ranking under 300, Mashable ranks as one of the world's largest websites. Times noted Mashable as one of the 25 best blogs in 2009, and has been described as "one stop shop" for social media. As of March 2012, it has over 2,775,000 Twitter followers and over 1,000,000 fans on Facebook.
URL: http://mashable.com/

196

MyStarbucksIdea.com
Mystarbucksidea.com was launched as an online community to promote communication between the company and its customers. The community is used by Starbucks to review and promote ideas. Customers can contact Starbucks representatives through multiple forums on the community site. The community has helped Starbuck incorporate customer feedback, promote new products, conduct polls to gauge popularity of its products, and interact more with its customers. With 3 million visitors and 60,000 ideas from customers, the community site has been a phenomenal success
URL: http://mystarbucksidea.force.com/

Nokia
Nokia Corporation is a Finnish multinational communications and information technology corporation that is headquartered in Espoo, Finland. Its principal products are mobile telephones and portable IT devices.
URL: http://www.nokia.com/

Nokia's Ovi Store
Ovi by Nokia was the brand for Nokia's Internet services. The Ovi services could be used from a mobile device, computer (through Nokia Ovi Suite), or via the web. Nokia focuses on five key service areas: Games, Maps, Media, Messaging, and Music. Nokia's aim with Ovi is to include third party developers, such as operators and third-party services like Yahoo's Flickr photo site.
URL: http://store.ovi.com/

OpenTable
OpenTable is an American public company that offers online real-time restaurant-reservation service. It was founded by Chuck Templeton in San Francisco, California, in 1998. Reservations are free to end users; the company charges restaurants monthly and per-reservation fees for their use of the system. In 1999, the website began operations serving a limited selection of restaurants in San Francisco. It has since expanded to cover 25,000 restaurants in most U.S. states as well as in several major international cities. Reservations can be made online through its website at opentable.com

URL: http://www.opentable.com/

PayPal
PayPal is a global e-commerce business allowing payments and money transfers to be made through the Internet. Online money transfers serve as electronic alternatives to paying with traditional paper methods, such as checks and money orders.
URL: https://www.paypal.com/

Pinterest
Pinterest is a pinboard-style photo-sharing website that allows users to create and manage theme-based image collections such as events, interests, and hobbies. Users can browse other pinboards for images, "re-pin" images to their own pinboards, or "like" photos.
URL: https://www.pinterest.com/

Quantcast
Quantcast is a digital advertising company, specializing in audience measurement and real-time advertising. Founded in 2006, the company is a pioneer of direct audience measurement technology.
URL: https://www.quantcast.com/

Research In Motion (See BlackBerry)

Second Life
Second Life is an online virtual world developed by Linden Lab. A number of free client programs, or Viewers, enable Second Life users to interact with each other through avatars (Also called Residents). Residents can explore the world (known as the grid), meet other residents, socialize, participate in individual and group activities, and create and trade virtual property and services with one another.
URL: http://secondlife.com/

Skype
Skype is a freemium voice-over-IP service and instant messaging client developed by the Microsoft Skype Division. The name originally derived from "sky" and "peer."
URL: http://www.skype.com/en/

Starbucks
Starbucks Corporation is an American global coffee company and coffeehouse chain based in Seattle, Washington.
URL: http://www.starbucks.com/

Tweet Adder
TweetAdder is an addon application that allows a twitter user to manage multiple Twitter accounts. Depending on the licenses they purchased, it can generate a massive fan base and the features include allowing a user to automatically follow and follow people and automatically generate tweets, and it also allows users to generate automatic messages to send to their followers.
URL: https://www.tweetadder.com/

Twitter
Twitter is an online social networking and microblogging service that enables users to send and read "tweets," which are text messages limited to 140 characters. Registered users can read and post tweets but unregistered users can only read them.
URL: https://twitter.com/

Windows Phone Marketplace
Windows Marketplace for Mobile was a service by Microsoft for its Windows Mobile platform that allows users to browse and download applications that have been developed by third parties. The service was available for use directly on Windows Mobile 6.x devices and on personal computers.
URL: http://www.windowsphone.com/en-us/store

Yelp
yelp.com, operated by Yelp, Inc., is a local directory service with social networking and user reviews. Yelp.com had more than 71 million monthly unique visitors as of January 2012. Yelp's revenue comes from local business advertising.
URL: http://www.yelp.com/

YouTube
YouTube is a video-sharing website, created by three former PayPal employees in February 2005, on which users can up-

load, view, and share videos. The company is based in San
Bruno, California, and uses Adobe Flash Video and HTML5
technology to display a wide variety of user-generated video
content, including movie clips, TV clips, and music videos, as
well as amateur content such as video blogging, short original
videos, and educational videos.
URL: http://www.youtube.com/

(Source: Wikipedia)

Index

catalyst, 5
catchy, 99, 119, 120
categories, 102, 103, 104, 105, 126
category, 141
Caucasian, 47
celebrity gossip, 15
cell phone, 23, 83, 139, 146
cell phone users, 142
cell phones, 19, 26, 108, 109, 110, 142, 152
CEO, 70, 117
challenge, 5, 96, 124
challenges, 120
changes, 96, 127
channel, 41, 79, 88
channels, 74
charts, 152
chat, 46
cheap, 59, 118
check boxes, 105
checklist, 147
cheerleaders, 85
chemotherapy, 6
chicken wings, 85
Children's Miracle Network Hospitals, 90
cinema, 3
Cisco, 75, 76, 77
Cisco Support Group, 76
citation, 141
citation management system, 112, 134
citation sites, 129, 138, 139
citations, 141
Clearwater, 85
click through rate, 12
click through rates, 32, 121
clicks, 121
client, 78, 126, 146
clientele, 9

clients, 9, 23, 25, 35, 38, 42, 45, 49, 54, 55, 61, 62, 96, 97, 98, 105, 110, 125, 126, 133, 136, 140, 141
clothes, 45
clothing, 104
clothing shop, 106
club, 116
clueless, 119
clutter, 37
Coca-Cola, 88, 130
cocktail, 6
coding, 116
coffee, 87
co-founder, 74
Coke Zero, 88
collect, 49, 105
college degree, 47, 123
color scheme, 97
comfortable, 139
comment capture page, 134
comment capture system, 112, 134
commerce, 4
commercial breaks, 139
commercial message, 36
commercials, 35, 36, 39
commitment, 63, 120
communication, 25, 42, 95
community, 66, 151
companies, 36, 123
companion, 145
company, 65, 70, 80, 87, 88, 134
company's mission statement, 151
company's policy, 63
comparison, 8, 118, 125
competing, 152
competition, 20, 61, 62, 63, 117, 119, 120, 121, 125,

D

E

F

free report, 15, 37
free tools, 55
free video, 37
freebie, 65
freebies, 16, 29, 108
freedom, 104
FREEPIZZA, 83
friend invites, 16
friends, 135, 138
frustrated, 16
frustration, 20
frustrations, 118
fulfill, 117
fun, 42, 46, 65, 76, 85, 119, 145
function, 39
functionalities, 10, 29, 112, 147
functionality, 23, 108, 110, 117, 145
functions, 98
fundamental, 7, 116
funding, 116
funds, 117
furniture, 104

G

gallons, 77
game, 36
game over, 116
games, 81
gap, 5, 146
garlic, 106
garner, 96, 105
Gartner, 20
gas, 77
gatekeepers, 118
gear symbol, 50
gem, 98

gender, 46
generate leads, 120
genesis, 120
geo-fence messages, 84
geographical location, 141
George Benckenstein, 36, 41
George Washington, 106
gift, 15
giveaways, 86
gizmos, 3
glimpse, 141
glitches, 118
global Internet traffic, 20
global market, 5
global scale, 10
globalization, 95
globe, 38
goals, 124
gold rush, 117
golden rule, 146
good reputation, 145
goods and services, 9
Google, 46, 118, 123, 127, 139, 141, 143, 144
Google authorship status, 141
Google Maps traffic, 135
graduate, 65
grand prize, 86
graphic designs, 106, 117, 123
graphics, 99
Great Depression, 69
grievances, 134
groundbreaking, 16
Groupon, 59
groups, 23, 39
grow, 53, 129, 137
growth, 22, 123
growth projection, 63
growth rate, 81

211

guarantee, 118, 145
guidance, 118
guidelines, 117, 152
guilty, 28
Gutenberg, 3, 4
gyms, 12

H

hair, 61
handbags, 98
hands, 110
handset sales, 81
handsets, 81
handy, 6, 60, 103
happy, 133, 136, 142, 146
hard work, 120
hardware, 81
Harvard Business Review, 134
hashtags, 55, 56
hassle, 9
Havana, 12
HD-Dolby Surround sound systems, 3
headaches, 118
headline, 51
health, 4
health and wealth, 12
health clubs, 12
help, 123
high converting, 119
high definition, 119
high end watches, 65
higher returns, 7, 39
hire, 127
Hispanic, 47
history of mankind, 3
hives, 109
home appliances, 35

home page tab, 99
homepage, 74
homework, 141
hook, 19
Hooters, 87
Hooters Girls, 85
Hooters Mobile Club, 85
Hooters Restaurant, 85
hope marketing, 59
hormone therapies, 6
hospitality, 21
hotel, 12
house, 138
Human Business Works, 70
human connection, 41
human experience, 5
humans, 5, 81
Hummingbird, 54, 55
hungry, 120
hurdle, 124
hurry, 120
hype, 27

I

icing on the cake, 137
icon, 119, 121, 127, 143
icon designs, 125
iconic, 106
icons, 118
idea, 116, 119
ideas, 95
identify, 45
image, 98
image galleries, 98, 152
image gallery, 106
imagery, 98
images, 10, 23, 52, 83
imagination, 5, 19, 35
I-Mode, 3

invoice, 125
iOS, 33
iPhone, 33, 79
IT professionals, 76
items, 102, 120, 147
iterative design, 16

J

James Bond, 65
JCPenney, 89
JetBlue, 78, 79, 80
jeweler, 106
jewelry brands, 21
JFK, 106
jigsaw puzzle, 6
journalist, 70

K

karaoke music, 110
karaoke song contests, 110
karma, 28
key media, 76
keyword, 56, 83
keyword analysis, 125
keyword list, 118
keyword research, 125
keywords, 55, 56, 89, 115
kick start, 106
kids, 47, 119
kiosks, 79
Kitchen Table Companies,
    70
knowledge, 30, 38, 42, 95,
    123
Koch, 45
KPIs, 63
Krishan Agarwal, 65

214

L

L.A. jewelry, 65
Lamborghini Gallardo, 125
land, 45
landing pages, 49
landing view, 51
landline phones, 81
landline telephone, 9, 25
landscape, 9
language, 52
laptops, 81, 97
last frontier, 5
launch, 77, 106, 126
launch expenses, 75
launch pages, 76
law of the jungle, 116
lawyer, 110
layout, 106
layouts, 99
lead, 39, 67
lead capture form, 147
lead capture forms, 145
lead generation, 7, 10, 28,
    96, 125, 133
lead generation system, 6
lead magnet, 5
leadership, 74
leads, 26, 27, 28, 49, 71,
    126
leaflets, 7
Lean Startup, 16
learn, 118
learning curve, 50
leeches, 141
legendary, 120
lemonade, 119
lethal, 106
letters, 7
level, 5
level of specifications, 125

M

S

stores, 73, 98
story, 120
strategic, 61
strategies, 106
strategy, 27, 55, 57, 115,
    122, 137
streaming, 3
streams, 133
streams of income, 135
street address, 8
strengths and weaknesses,
    121
strike, 126
stringent, 117
struggle, 8, 120
student discounts, 95
studies, 25, 132
study, 20
stylists, 74
subatomic, 152
subcategories, 103, 104
submenus, 102, 104
submission rate, 118
submit, 118
submit button, 106
subscribe, 61
subscription, 41
substantial, 82
subterfuges, 8
subtitled movies, 3
subtle, 52
subway, 119
succeed, 116
success, 45, 129
successful, 115, 116
successful campaign, 152
successful ROI campaigns,
    91
Super Bowl, 36, 87
super offer, 8
supercharge sales, 6

superfans programmes, 73
superior, 39
supermarkets, 95
supplements, 12
supply, 124
support, 42, 123
supporter, 70
surf habits, 125
Surfcomber Hotel, 86
surge, 7, 72
survey, 21, 106
surveys, 141
Swarn Badge, 69
sweet spot, 145
Symphony, 77
synergetic, 129, 137
synergetic effect, 137

T

tab, 99, 101, 103, 104, 107,
    110, 112
tables, 9, 151
tablet PCs, 81
tablet usage, 10
tablets, 19
takeaway company, 73
Tamagotchi, 3
tangible, 8
TapJoy, 31
tap-to-call, 99, 147
tap-to-map, 147
target, 39, 48
target area, 54
target audience, 7, 12, 16,
    30, 46, 47, 52, 55, 82, 97,
    105, 109, 115, 117, 120,
    124, 125, 148
target audiences, 37, 74
targeted, 84

trigger, 98
trillion, 81
trivial, 49
trucks, 35
trust, 41, 42, 60, 97, 132, 146
T-shirts, 106
tunings, 52
turbo-charge, 137
tutorials, 57
TV, 3, 9, 10, 12, 14, 25, 35, 82, 98, 106, 115, 123, 139
TV ads, 39
TV sets, 81
TV show, 139
tweak, 14, 39, 53, 119
tweaks, 127
tweet, 71, 79, 98, 109
Tweet Adder, 54, 55
tweets, 55, 56, 62, 71, 98
Twellow.com, 55
twist, 139
Twitter, 15, 27, 28, 46, 54, 56, 57, 66, 69, 71, 74, 77, 78, 79, 80, 109, 110
Twitter account, 46, 71
Twitter audience, 55
Twitter campaign, 69, 80
Twitter followers, 69
Twitterlocal.net, 55
Twittersearch.com, 66
Twollow.com, 56
type, 148

U

Uber, 17
Uber User Internet Addicts, 76
UI, 97

UK, 72, 144
Uncle Kracker, 86
understanding, 42, 116
unique, 42
unique attributes, 9
unique selling proposition, 119, 120
unique specifications, 98, 125
unique users, 81
unison, 137
units, 9, 129
unsolicited ads, 38
update, 37
updates, 41, 52, 61, 65
upgrade, 32
upgrades, 29
uphill battle, 118
upper-hand, 152
up-sell, 32, 135
up-sells, 133
URL, 53, 148, 150
URLs, 91
usage, 33, 61
usage duration, 122
USC MBA, 65
use, 122
usefulness, 109, 120
user, 53, 116, 119
user experience, 30, 117, 118
user friendly, 119
user generated content, 40
User personas, 31
user's experience, 97
user-friendly, 96
user-friendly app, 96
usernames, 17
users, 28, 40, 46, 81, 106, 118, 143
users' attention, 96

website, 6, 19, 22, 30, 67,
    71, 80, 99, 112, 125, 142,
    143, 144, 145
website metadata, 141
website SEO, 141
websites, 5, 20, 21, 22, 40,
    54, 98, 109, 143, 145, 168
weight, 53
well-designed, 97
West Palm Beach, 12
white paper, 78
white papers, 77
widget, 76
Wild West, 116
wind, 126
window, 50
Windows Phone
    Marketplace, 33
wine, 15, 46
wine connoisseur, 52
wine forums, 46
wine shop, 46
wines, 102
Wisconsin, 69
wise, 98
witness accounts, 110
witnesses, 110
word, 141

word of mouth, 74
word of mouth
    advertisement, 7, 8
word of mouth advertising,
    14, 23, 41, 80, 138
word-of-mouth stir, 151
WordPress, 147
words, 119
work, 36, 118, 125
work relationship, 123
worst case scenario, 118
worth, 120, 126, 135
worthy, 118
wrongs, 134

Y

Yellow Pages, 123, 139
Yelp, 74, 112
YouTube, 109

Z

zip code, 84

About The Author

Author, consultant, Internet marketer pro, Maurice Ufituwe is an entrepreneur with a degree in MBA who specializes in helping entrepreneurs and small businesses gain a competitive advantage in their local market — both online and off. He helps these businesses get "found" online, ensures that they never run out of leads, and helps them transform their potential clients into lifetime customers (and raving fans!).

He grew up in many cultures on both sides of the Atlantic; he is fluent in English, French, and German and he has no problem promoting your business and brand across borders despite the language barriers and geographical locations.

His passion for the Internet and the subsequent rise of Mobile app began in early 1996 with a few ads he discovered in a trade magazine that showed how to run ads for local businesses on the World Wide Web; at a time when barely few people knew what "Internet" was and how to spell it right. He is convinced that Mobile app will bridge the gaps among cultures, create an abundance of wealth, foster knowledge and education around the world.

Made in the USA
Monee, IL
05 July 2022

99127823R00138